A Complete Guide to
Canoeing

CARL MONK
JEROME KNAP

A Complete Guide to Canoeing

CARL MONK
JEROME KNAP

A manual on technique and equipment and the best canoeing routes in North America

PAGURIAN PRESS LIMITED
TORONTO

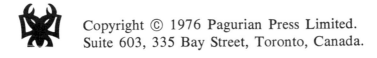
ISBN 0-88932-023-3 cloth
0-919364-98-5 paper
Printed and Bound in the United States of America

Contents

Introduction

It is difficult to completely comprehend the historical significance of the canoe. Without it, it is unlikely that La Salle would ever have made his epic journey down the Mississippi to claim what was later termed the "Louisiana Purchase" for the King of France. It is unlikely that the La Verendrye brothers would have traveled to Lake Winnipeg to open the gateway to the west. And, of course, the canoe allowed Mackenzie to travel to the Arctic Ocean and later to the Pacific some years before Lewis and Clark made their epic journey overland.

Without the canoe, the fur trade would have been much more difficult. And there is no doubt that it was the furs — particularly the beaver — that created the commercial impetus for much of the European exploration on this continent, once the Europeans had concluded that this new land held no easy passage to China.

The men who paddled canoes during the early era were the greatest canoeists ever. We, modern voyageurs, pale beside them. We can never hope to match their spirit, savvy, or stamina. Yet one does not need to compete with the voyageurs of old to enjoy the freedom and bounty of the canoe. Many rivers still flow unfettered by dams; much wilderness is left untouched by farms, mines, settlements, or highways. And even where wilderness has been conquered, a canoeist can still find water in which to wet his paddle, as some modern-day voyageurs have discovered in their trips around the waterfronts of big cities or on man-made canals and lakes.

The modern voyageur who wants to feel his paddle bite the water and to send his canoe gliding will always find a place.

Vive le voyageur!

PART I
The Canoe

The birch bark canoe saw its greatest use among Indian tribes east of the Mississippi.

CHAPTER 1

The Romance of the Canoe

The canoe is a symbol of wilderness — of rivers running free. It is an ideal craft with which to penetrate the wilderness; an ideal craft with which to run wild rivers. The early canoeists were unfettered people — full of independence, self reliance, adventure, and courage. They were physically tough, and their souls sang with a "joie de vie."

The legacy of the canoe is intrinsically tied in with the history and early commerce of the northern half of this continent, Canada in particular. Indeed the early history of Canada is almost a series of ever longer and bolder canoe trips into the heart of this continent. When steam and rail came into use the canoe still continued to be the best and easiest method for travel into remote areas — even for Canadian governors, several of whom made long and exhausting canoe trips into the hinterlands of their territories.

Even today, in the era of float planes, the canoe is still useful for trappers, prospectors, geologists, surveyors, forest rangers, and timber cruisers from Newfoundland to Alaska.

The Indian Canoe

We in North America tend to view the canoe as "our" invention, an invention of the North American Indian. This is not so. The canoe was "invented" by many peoples in many parts of the world — Africa, Asia, South America, and the islands of the South Pacific, the only differences being in the method of construction. The river tribes of Africa, the aboriginals of Asia, the Polynesians, the Paupaus, the Indians of South America, and

11

The west coast tribes built large dugout canoes, and were expert mariners. Dugout canoes are also used in Africa, South America, and Polynesia.

even those of the North American Pacific coast, used dugout canoes. Eastern American Indians and those in the western mountains, on the other hand, made their canoes out of bark. We tend to think of birch-bark canoes as typical, yet bark from at least 10 or 12 other species of trees was also used. The Iroquois, for example, commonly made canoes of elm bark, while the Kootneys and other mountain tribes of British Columbia used pine. However, the birch-bark canoe was the most widely used because the white birch or paper birch grows widely across the northern portion of this continent, and because it is easily peeled, fairly pliable when wet, and surprisingly durable.

All bark canoes had one feature in common. They were light and easy to handle, both in and out of the water. They were as

The Montagnis of Quebec built birch-bark canoes right up to this century.

ideal for traveling "up the little rivers as up the large ones" as Samuel de Champlain once put it. Indeed, until the advent of cedar and canvas, and later of aluminum and fiberglass, bark was the unsurpassed material for canoe construction.

It is difficult to say which Indian nations and tribes were the best canoeists or which built the best canoes. Undoubtedly the best bark canoes were built by the eastern or northern tribes. The plains Indians, such as the Blackfeet, scorned the canoe. When the white man arrived on their land, they were already horsemen.

Father Galinue, a cartographer who traveled with the explorer La Salle, became an expert canoeist. He claimed that the

13

Algonquins whose canoes lasted for 5 or 6 years, made better canoes than the Iroquois. Francis Parkman called the Huron canoes "masterpieces of Indian handiwork." Diamond Jenness, in his book *Indians of Canada* (Queen's Printer, 1960), lists the Micmacs, the Algonquins, the Hurons (particularly the Ottawas), and the Swampy Crees as being the best canoeists. But Sir George Simpson, the governor of the Hudson Bay Company after it had amalgamated with the North West Company in 1821, used Iroquois canoeists on all his travels in the Canadian north and west, having great faith in their ability with a paddle and on a portage.

The Slave and Dogrib Indians of the far north built birch-bark canoes with spruce frames. These were rather small, usually made for only one man. Mackenzie once remarked that their canoes were agile and easy to handle.

The Interior Solish made pine canoes with sharp noses and stems running underwater, similar to the canoes made by the natives around the Amur River in eastern Siberia. These Interior Solish canoes were about 15 feet long, made of cedar frames covered with spruce or pine bark turned inside out, so that the smooth inner surface of the bark faced the water.

Of the coastal Indians, the Haidas of the Queen Charlotte Islands were among the best whalers and mariners on the Pacific coast. They did not hesitate to venture from sight of land on their whaling expeditions. Probably all the coastal tribes in their dugout canoes were expert canoeists, although not all used large war canoes. In fact, most were small craft for two to four men, used mainly for fishing and sealing.

The first white man to see canoes was, of course, Columbus, who saw those of the Carib Indians. The name canoe reportedly comes from the Carib word "kanawa." But linguistically the word can be traced even further, to the old Siberian and Mongolian languages where similar terms mean "a boat with pointed ends."

Probably the first white man to see an Indian birch-bark canoe was John Cabot in 1497 when he dropped anchor off the coast of Cape Breton Island where the Micmac Indians were expert canoeists. But nothing exists of Cabot's thoughts about this Indian vessel. It took another century, when the great era of exploration started, for the canoe's virtues to be appreciated by the white man.

The Canoe and Exploration

The first European explorer to use and write about the birch-bark canoe was Samuel de Champlain. He was quick to admit that it was a far better craft for Canadian exploration than the skiff in which he had traveled to reach what is now known as the Lachine Rapids.

"With the canoes of the savages" Champlain wrote in 1603, "one may travel freely and quickly throughout the country as well up the little rivers as up the large ones."

In the year 1608, Champlain joined a war party of Huron, Algonquin, and some Montagnais Indians against the Iroquois. They traveled south on the Richelieu River, eventually reaching a large lake which Champlain named after himself. What impressed him most was the speed with which they traveled. ". . . every day we made 25 to 30 leagues in their canoes," he wrote. In 1615 he and Etienne Brule traveled by canoe up the Ottawa River and from there to Lake Huron via the Mattawa and French River systems. On this trip the canoe route to the west was laid open and the great period of exploration and fur trade began.

In 1660, Jean Nicolet canoed across Lake Michigan and reached Green Bay, the Fox River, and Lake Winnebago. A dozen years later Radison and de Grosselliers paddled northward from Lake Superior to the headwaters of the Albany River and from there into Hudson Bay. When they returned to Three Rivers, they brought with them 360 canoes laden with furs. Pierre de Voyer, the French governor at Quebec, who had forbidden them to take such journeys, fined the two explorers one-third of their furs. As a result, they switched their allegiance to the English, and, on visiting England, told King Charles of the unlimited wealth in furs waiting to be traded in the wilderness around Hudson Bay.

In 1673, Count Frontenac, governor of New France, sent Louis Joliet and Father Marquette, a Jesuit, westward to find the giant river of the west. They left in two birch-bark canoes on May 17 and reached the Mississippi a month later. Joliet returned to Lachine four months later, having covered 2400 miles. An expert canoeist, he claimed that 50 portages were needed to make the journey upstream — westward; to return, only 15 were needed if one were skilled enough in running rapids.

It was not until 1682 that La Salle, with a party of 54 men, canoed down the Mississippi. Leaving Fort Frontenac on Lake Ontario, they canoed westward through the Great Lakes to Illinois, and from there inland to the Mississippi River and south as far as the Gulf of Mexico. Along the way the party visited numerous Indian villages, and La Salle claimed the land for the King of France. This epic journey still stands as one of the most audacious canoe trips of all time.

For the next hundred years, canoe exploration turned to the Canadian west. It was La Verendrye who first canoed from Lake Superior to Lake of the Woods, where one of his sons was killed by the Sioux. His two other sons, François and Pierre, continued exploring westward establishing forts on Lake Winnipeg, Lake Manitoba, the Red River, and finally the Assiniboine River.

This bold move enraged the Hudson Bay Company. Fearing that the French forts in Manitoba would stop the Indians from going northward to their trading posts on Hudson Bay, the company began to send flotillas of canoes westward on the big rivers that flow to Hudson Bay. By this time the French had already established posts on the Saskatchewan River. In spite of this, Hudson Bay Company employees, such as Curry Finlay, Frobisher, Paterson, Alexander Henry, and even such independent traders as Peter Pond, a Connecticut Yankee, continued their canoe travels on the western rivers.

A new, and perhaps the greatest, era of canoeing began with the formation in Montreal of the North West Company in 1783. In 1789, Alexander Mackenzie, an officer of the company, left Fort Chipawayon on Lake Athabaska and canoed down the river that later bore his name — the Mackenzie. He wanted to reach the Pacific Ocean. His canoe was a 32-foot birch-bark craft. On reaching the ocean, Mackenzie saw that it was not the Pacific but the "Frozen Ocean" of the north. His round-trip of over 2000 miles took 102 days to complete.

16

Up to then, no white man had crossed the Rocky Mountains. But in 1793, Alexander Mackenzie traveled over the Peace River Pass and re-launched his canoe on the Blackwater River. From there he made his way to an Indian village on the Bella Coola, near the coast, having just missed meeting George Vancouver, who was exploring the British Columbia coast from the sea. The next man to cross the Rockies was David Thompson, a surveyor in the employ of the North West Company. Thompson chose a different route. He canoed up the Saskatchewan River to the Howse Pass. There he abandoned his canoes and traveled on horses purchased from the Indians. On reaching the Columbia River, the party camped and built new canoes with which they traveled to Astoria at the mouth of the Columbia.

The Voyageurs

The romance of the canoe does not just stem from the era of exploration. The incredible journeys of the voyageurs add immensely to the history of canoe travel. These adventurers were divided into two groups: the Porkeaters or Comers and Goers, and the North Men or Winterers.

The Porkeaters paddled from Montreal each spring to Grand Portage, now the extreme northeastern tip of Minnesota. Their 500-pound canoes were 25 to 40 feet long, laden with massive cargoes of rum and trade goods. In Grand Portage they camped and waited for the North Men to come from as far north as Fort Chipawayon on Lake Athabaska through the vast wilderness of Canada's north west. The canoes of the North Men were smaller — 22 feet in length, the maximum size for river travel. The North Men brought with them cargoes of fur. At Grand Portage they switched cargoes and each party began the return journey.

The Porkeaters were mostly Quebeckers, while the North Men were frequently part Indian, scions of the union of early Quebec voyageurs and Indian women. The North Men were the elite of the voyageurs. To them, unexplored territories, dangerous rapids, and long portages were shrugged off as routine. On long portages each man carried two 90-pound packs; on short portages some carried more. And they always trotted, never walked. What made this even more remarkable is that they were physi-

The voyageurs had a Gallic zest for life which they showed in the color of their dress, their jokes and laughter, and most of all their songs.

cally small men. Large men took up too much space in the canoes, space that was needed for trade goods.

Their day started before daybreak and lasted until dark. They sometimes paddled 80 miles in one day. Traditionally they crossed the huge Lake Winnipeg in an orgy of self endurance. And even after they had beached their canoes, the day's work was not over. They had to cook their meals and gum the frail canoes to stop leaks.

It was said of the voyageurs that they were "obsessed with a desire to be first." Every canoe wanted to be in the lead. They paddled at full speed at all times. Those that did not drown or were not killed in accidents were old men at forty, worn out by the rigors of their occupation.

The Porkeaters were of a different temperament. They were skillful navigators, accustomed to big waters. Their journeys were less perilous, less physically demanding, and less frenzied. They had the Gallic zest for life which they showed in the color of their dress, in their jokes and laughter, and, most of all, in their songs.

R. M. Ballantyne, who canoed from Norway House on Hudson Bay to Lake of the Woods and from there eastward to Lachine in Quebec, describes the fur brigades, including the

The voyageurs often traveled 80 miles per day, stopping only at night to rest under their long birch-bark canoes.

exhilarating songs of the voyageurs, in greater detail than any other early traveler. He states that every summer no less than 10 brigades departed, each numbering 20 or more canoes. "I have seen the canoes sweep around a promontory suddenly and burst upon my view, while at the same moment the wild romantic song of the voyageurs, as they plied their brisk paddles, struck upon my ear," he wrote. "And with hearts joyful at the happy termination of their trials and privations, sang, with all the force of three hundred manly voices, one of their lively airs which swelled out in the rich tones of many a mellow voice." (*Hudson Bay,* Blackwoods, 1850).

Even Washington Irving commented in his book, *Astoria* (Knickerbocker Press, 1836) on the singing of the voyageurs. "The steersman often sings an old traditionary French song with some regular burden in which they all join, keeping time with their oars," he wrote. "The Canadian waters are vocal with these little French *chansons* that have been echoed from mouth to mouth and transmitted from father to son from the earliest days of the colony."

The musical nature of the voyageurs was exploited by John Jacob Astor to publicize his American Fur Company. While a

19

guest of the Beaver Club in Montreal, Astor arranged for a crew of Canadian voyageurs to paddle to Lake Champlain and from there down the Hudson River, singing their *chansons,* all the way to New York.

Today, the songs that the voyageurs sang to paddle by are treasures of musical folklore. Some would be considered ribald even in our liberated age.

CHAPTER 2

Anatomy of a Canoe

Before we can talk about canoes and canoeing, we must understand what the canoe is all about, in terms of form and function.

No other boat can approach the canoe in efficiency in river or lake travel. As we will learn, the canoe can be paddled, poled, rowed, powered by motor and even by sail. What other water craft offers such versatility? And, to boot, it has great weight-carrying ability.

The canoe has virtues that no other boat possesses. The paddler faces forward and sees exactly where he is going. In most other small craft, the oarsman faces the back of the boat. Another virtue is that it can be carried easily. This is not solely because of its light weight (many small boats are light) but because of its long, slim shape. A man can lift it to his shoulders and walk with it, threading his way among underbrush if necessary, which is the reason for the canoe's illustrious history in the exploration of this continent.

The long, slim shape of the canoe also allows it to slip easily through the water. It offers comparatively little resistance, so it is easy to propel and maneuver.

Canoes come in a variety of shapes and sizes because the size of the canoe, to a large degree, determines its cargo capacity or the weight of cargo that it can safely carry. The shape determines where the canoe will be used and for what. For example,

21

ANATOMY OF A CANOE

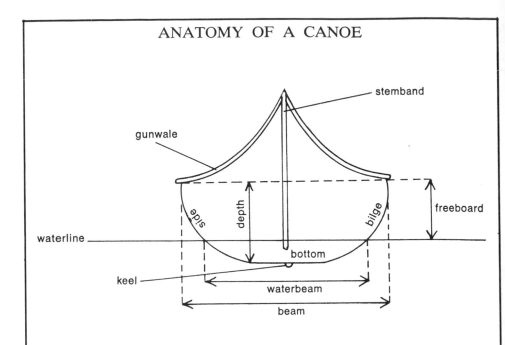

Fig. 1

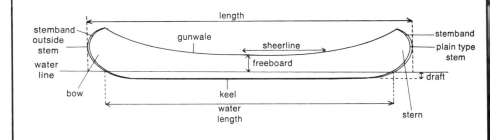

Fig. 2

ANATOMY OF A CANOE (Cont'd.)

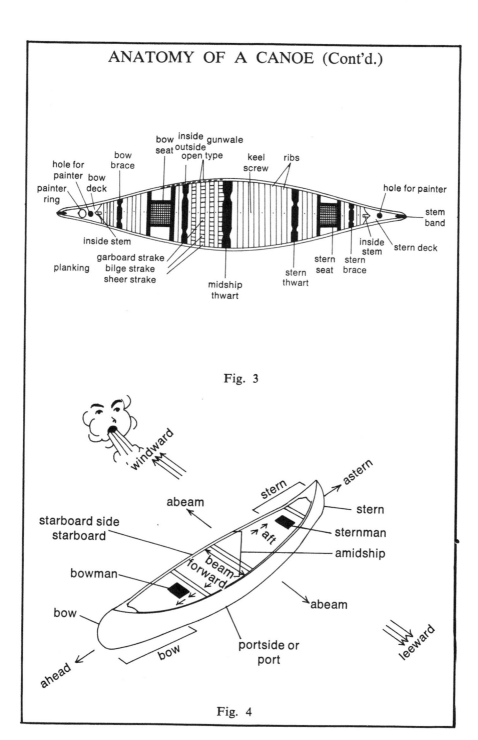

Fig. 3

Fig. 4

canoes designed primarily for lake travel are different from those designed for fast rivers. Shape also has some bearing on the cargo capacity.

However, regardless of the task for which the canoe has been designed, all have some basic features in common. To understand the canoe, one must first understand its anatomy.

CHAPTER 3

Choosing a Canoe

When a tyro canoeist decides to buy a canoe, he wonders what size and material it should be. Seldom does he give any thought to the canoe's shape, particularly the shape of the hull. We admit that size is an important consideration. The size determines, in part, where the canoe will be used and for what. But so does the shape of the hull. Actually, the material from which the canoe is constructed plays only a minor role in the craft's efficiency. Birch-bark canoes, after all, were used under all the conditions that today's aluminum, fiberglass, or wood and canvas canoes are subjected to. Canoeing conditions have not changed much. If anything, they are less rigorous and demanding. Many of our wild rivers have been tamed and fettered by dams, and few canoes today are used on long, hazardous voyages starting from spring breakup until late in the fall.

All Shapes

The shape of a canoe's hull has a direct bearing on its function, and on where and how it should ideally be used. For example, one with a round bottom is faster and responds quicker to the paddle than one of equal weight and length, but with a flat bottom. On the other hand, a flat-bottomed canoe is more stable because it floats above the stream of moving water. Its wider surface area minimizes any sideways motion. It also offers more resistance to water. All these characteristics lend it stability and safety. Flat-bottomed canoes also provide more room for carrying loads.

A canoe with a round bottom settles down into the water flow a bit more, but the surface area that actually meets with the surface tension of the water is less than in a flat-bottomed canoe. This puts less drag on the canoe, and gives it more speed and easier maneuverability. To put it another way, there is less friction.

As a result, canoes designed primarily for fast rivers — for white-water travel — generally have rounded bottoms for maximum maneuverability. Racing canoes also have round bottoms because they are designed for speed.

The Indians recognized the importance of hull shape. The Great Lakes tribes built their canoes with fairly flat bottoms while the Montagnais and the Crees built theirs with round bottoms for river travel. Indeed, the ideal canoe for river travel should have a bit of a crooked shape, with an upswept keel line at both ends, (like the early Montagnais canoes) so that it can pivot around obstructions in rapids.

Because the round-bottomed canoe has less friction on water, it is not as stable and consequently is not as safe for the novice. It is also less resistant to wind. (Wind can push it around more easily.) This is so because round-bottomed river canoes do not have keels. A keel makes a canoe less maneuverable, but we will have more to say about keels and their purpose later.

There is no doubt that flat-bottomed canoes are the work horses — the Fords, Chevrolets, and Volkswagens — of canoeing. They are the logical choice for most canoeists. Their cargo capacity makes them ideal for canoe tripping. Their stability and safety makes them ideal for novices. Canoes with round bottoms, on the other hand, are the "sport" models — the Corvettes and Jaguars — of canoeing. They are for river running and for shooting white waters which, as we will repeat later, are pastimes for experts.

The taper of the hull also has a bearing on the canoe's function. A canoe with a sharp taper towards the bow and stern is easier to paddle and drive ahead; it is much faster. It knifes through the surface tension of the water more easily than a canoe with a slow-tapering bow. Also, because there is less friction involved, such a canoe is easier to maneuver. But again, this type

26

The taper of the hull has a bearing on a canoe's function. The racing canoe in the foreground has a fast taper and is rather narrow. The touring canoe in the background has a slower taper and is a bit wider.

is less stable and seaworthy. In rough seas it tends to cut through waves rather than ride over them. A fast taper is basically a racing adaptation. All racing canoes are fast-tapered, and some are even very narrow amidship. Probably the greatest proponent of the fast-tapered hull shape is Ralph Sawyer, whose Sawyer Canoe Company is a leading builder of racing canoes.

Avoid a canoe with a sharp taper for basic canoeing, particularly if you have long-distance canoe tripping in mind. The fast taper cuts down on cargo capacity and in high seas when such a canoe is heavily laden, waves splash over it because, as we pointed out earlier, the bow knifes into the waves instead of riding over them. Basically it is an ideal choice for those who enjoy speed and river travel but do not particularly want to go on long canoe trips. It is suitable only for trips of a few days'

A wide, flat bottom on a canoe gives the craft stability. But if the bottom is very wide, as on this Sportspal, the canoe loses maneuverability.

duration when a minimum of gear is needed. However, with today's compact and light camping equipment, designed primarily for backpacking, and with the availabality of light, dehydrated foods, a canoe tripper can travel light and still be well equipped. One advantage of fast-taper canoes is that they are lighter than the slow-taper canoes of the same material and length. They are trimmer, and have less material in them.

The only other variable in the shape of a canoe is its profile. Many older canoes had fairly high peaks fore and aft. These added grace and beauty to the craft, but they made it highly wind resistant. Even a small breeze could push against the canoe with surprising force. Today, there is a revival of high peaks fore and aft, but only to attract the less knowledgeable purchaser. It makes the canoe look more traditional. (After all, the big freighter canoes of the early voyageurs had high peaks.) We advise that you pick a canoe with a lower profile that is more utilitarian. Canoes with high peaks are fine for small, sheltered waters, but sooner or later you will get caught in strong winds on the other side of the lake. And then what?

Keels and Their Purpose

The primary purpose of a keel is to prevent side-drift or side-slip on windswept lakes. A canoe with a keel can be kept on course much better than one without one. On the other hand, a keel is a handicap in fast water. A canoe with a keel becomes less maneuverable — sluggish to side pushes or strokes away from obstructions and through rapids. The keel also gives the current something to grab onto or push against.

River canoes with round bottoms never have keels, while canoes for open water always do. The problem is that most canoes are used on both rivers and lakes. This necessitates a compromise.

Wood-and-canvas canoes generally have a keel that is about ⅞ inches deep and about ¾ inches thick. The keels on aluminum canoes are about the same depth, but are thinner and sharper. Fiberglass canoes have keels that are molded in as longitudinal ridges or bulges. In the case of fiberglass canoes, these ridge or bulge-like keels give strength and rigidity to the hull.

Probably the best keel for a canoe meant for river and lake travel is the so-called "shoe keel." It is only about ⅝ inches deep, but is quite wide — generally from 2 to 4 inches. Its shallow depth allows the canoe to be fairly easily maneuvered in fast water, while slowing the wind drift on open water.

The width of the shoe keel also gives the bottom of the canoe a high degree of protection from rocks and gravel. For this reason a keel is a good bet on wood-and-canvas canoes or even on those of very light aluminum. Many canoe builders offer shoe keels as an extra option. Actually, all keels protect the canoe somewhat, and add strength and rigidity to the hull, but the wider the keel, the more protection, strength, and rigidity it gives.

Wood-and-canvas canoes frequently have bilge keels added to the bottom. These are simply smaller, shorter keels lying parallel, one on each side, of the standard keel. They are generally added to the canoe by the owner, but are sometimes put on by the canoe builder, particularly if the canoe is custom built. The length, thickness, and depth of bilge keels varies depending on the ideas of the owner. We have seen them up to 2 inches deep and 6 or 7 feet long.

The main purpose of these keels is to protect the bottom of the canoe. For this reason they were often used by trappers so that the canoe could be dragged over beaver dams and other obstructions.

Bilge keels, of course, make a canoe very sluggish to handle and hard to maneuver in fast water, but they also slow down wind drift.

Some fiberglass canoes come with molded bilge keels, but these are generally too short and shallow to protect the canoe from scrapes. Their main purpose is to give extra strength and rigidity to the hull. One disadvantage is that they act as troughs for holding debris and water.

What Length?

"How long a canoe should I buy?" is an often-asked question. The answer depends primarily on what kind of canoeing you want to do.

The length of a canoe has a bearing on its load capacity. For example, only long canoes are suitable for long canoe trips. Yet this is not the whole story. There are a number of other factors that have a bearing on cargo capacity as well. The width of the beam is one, the depth of the canoe is another. Obviously the deeper the canoe, the greater its load capacity. For example, a 16-foot canoe with a 34-inch beam width and a 12-inch depth will have a total load capacity of 600 pounds. A canoe of the same length and width but with a 14-inch depth will have a total load capacity of 850 pounds.

Advice on how long or big a canoe should be can be misleading. One canoeing book advises to get the longest canoe that you can lift and carry. This is a good rule of thumb for a canoe tripper because there are a number of different 18-foot canoes on the market that can easily be lifted and carried by one man. But an 18-foot canoe would be too cumbersome for trout fishing or duck hunting on small, log-infested beaver ponds. Such a canoe would not be ideal for small, shallow streams either. And an 18-foot canoe would not be a good choice for a man who likes to paddle alone. For one man, it is too long to handle easily.

For general canoe tripping, we recommend canoes 16 to 18 feet long, 34 to 37 inches wide at the beam, and 12 to 15 inches deep. A pair of canoe trippers will find a 16-foot canoe adequate for even a month-long canoe trip. A couple with two children would find an 18-foot canoe a better bet.

Canoes of 14 or 15 feet are, in our opinion, in-between lengths. They are too long to be one-man canoes and too short for long canoe trips with two people (unless they have a wider-than-normal beam which increases cargo capacity. They are usually chosen by tyros because they seem more maneuverable and lighter, and are a good bet for casual paddling or even river running. They may even be a good bet for fishing. But they are not meant for carrying cargo. And as soon as the beam is widened to increase cargo capacity, maneuverability and lightness are lost.

Canoes of 12 or 13 feet in length are primarily one-man crafts. Their major use is by trappers and canoe trippers who like to travel alone. A 12-foot canoe with a 32-inch beam can easily carry one man and all the gear and provisions he will need for a month-long trip into the wilderness.

Canoes under 12 feet in length, such as the 10½-foot Rushton of the Old Town Canoe Company, are essentially novelty items — playthings for experts.

The accompanying table gives an idea of maximum cargo capacities for canoes of various lengths, depths, and widths of beam.

Length (feet)	Beam width (inches)	Depth (inches)	Cargo capacity (pounds)
11	33	12	300
12	32	12	400
13	35	12	600
14	32	12	500
14	35	13	600
15	34	12	700
15	36	12	750
15	36	14	800
16	34	12	600
16	36	12	700
16	35	13	700
17	36	13	750
17	37	14½	900
18	37	13	1000
18	38	15	1100
20	39	15	1400
22	39	15	1600
24	40	15	1700
26	40	15	1900

What Material?

A century and a half ago, choosing a canoe was a simple task. The canoeist had only the length and the type of bottom to decide upon. Both considerations were largely determined by where the canoe would be used — on lakes or rivers — and for what purpose — canoe tripping, fishing, or river running. Regardless of what length he chose and whether the bottom was round or flat, the canoe was made of wood-and-canvas; wood in the form of thin cedar strips, or birch bark if he could find an Indian craftsman who still knew how to make one.

Today, the canoeist has other materials to choose from — aluminum, fiberglass, ABS plastic and other synthetics, plus of course, wood-and-canvas, cedar strip, and even birch bark (birch-bark canoes are enjoying a revival). There is no question that aluminum and synthetic materials have captured much of

Aluminum, fiberglass, and wood and canvas are the most popular materials for canoe building. But birch barks are still made for those with nostalgia in their souls.

the market. They are materials of the 20th century, requiring comparatively little hand labor in the canoe's manufacture. However, wood-and-canvas canoes are still popular among purists who view aluminum and the synthetics as an abomination of the canoe-making trade. Yet all have their advantages and disadvantages. Each can do something that the others cannot and each has a quality that the others lack.

Wood. Boating and canoeing writers have been prophesying the death of the wood-and-canvas canoe for a decade or two, all prematurely. The wood-and-fabric canoe still has a following and probably always will have. It has an aesthetic charm that neither fiberglass nor aluminum can match. The traditions of modern canoeing were founded on wood-and-fabric canoes. The logic in this, if there is one, is the same as preferring flyrods of split bamboo to those of fiberglass. There are many outdoorsmen who follow traditions, not because of any dogma but because these traditions add richness to their pursuits.

Also, wood-and-cloth canoes are products of hand craftsmanship, of labor lovingly performed, and there are people who will willingly pay more for a hand-crafted item than for one that has been mass-produced on an assembly line, even if the assembly-line model is just as utilitarian. However, the wood-and-canvas canoe has more to offer than just aesthetics and tradition. It is much quieter than aluminum; even quieter than fiberglass. It can slip along a river or lake almost noiselessly, making it the ideal craft for hunting or wildlife photography. It is cooler in summer, while aluminum and fiberglass radiate heat and throw it back into the canoeist's face. Conversely, it is warmer in cold weather. Wood always feels warmer to the touch than metal or fiberglass.

The wood-and-cloth canoe is less buoyant than aluminum. For this reason it is less susceptible to wind. It also seems to settle better on the water. But perhaps most important of all is its flotation quality. It floats well even when capsized or full of water. It needs no flotation material or air chambers. A wood-and-cloth canoe, even when fully awash, can still support at least one paddler inside and several more clinging to its sides.

Much has been written about the so-called fragility of the wood-and-canvas canoe. While there is no dispute that both aluminum and fiberglass are stronger materials, the wood-and-canvas canoe is surprisingly tough and sturdy. It slides off rocks with relative ease. It takes repeated blows or a head-on collision with a sharp rock to puncture the canvas and rupture the planking. The ribs are even harder to crack.

The biggest problem with a wood-and-canvas canoe is maintenance. This is one reason why canoe liveries, canoeing out-fitters, and fishing lodges have switched almost universally to aluminum or fiberglass. Stripping, sanding, painting, and varnishing a fleet of canoes each spring is a time-consuming and expensive task.

The wood-and-cloth canoe has other disadvantages. Being more fragile than aluminum or fiberglass, it may not be the ideal craft for tyro canoeists. This disadvantage is largely offset by the fact that emergency field repairs can be easily made on it. (See Chapter 15.)

It is not always true that wood-and-canvas canoes are heavier than aluminum. In fact, ultra-light canoes have been constructed using planking only 1/8 inches thick and Dacron cloth instead of canvas. But one thing is certain: a wood-and-canvas canoe gets heavier each spring when the anual coat of varnish is added.

It is also susceptible to rot and mildew, which means it must be properly stored when not in use, particularly during the winter. Also, if left in the hot summer sun for long periods of time, the paint cracks and chips. But perhaps the biggest disadvantage of a wood-and-canvas canoe is its cost. It can cost twice as much as fiberglass.

There are other small features in its favor. The open gunwale (the space between the ribs along the edge of the canoe at the top) is one. The reason for this open space is to facilitate fast draining when the canoe is overturned on shore. Canoes made of metal and synthetic fibers have solid gunwales with holes in them for draining, but these never work as well because they frequently become clogged with twigs, dirt, and other debris.

While on the subject of wood-and-canvas canoes, let us discuss wood canoes made of cedar planking. These are rarely encountered today, but they are among the most attractive canoes made. They are ribbed and planked like conventional canoes, but instead of being covered by canvas, are varnished, or, more recently, coated with urethane.

Metal. Ten years ago aluminum canoes dominated the canoeing scene. The golden age of the wood-and-canvas canoe was over, fiberglass canoes had not yet established their fine reputation. The aluminum canoe is still very popular and for a good reason: it is durable. You can drag it over beaver dams and rock-lined shallows. You can run it up on gravel beaches and bounce it off rocks in fast water. The damage will be negligible — perhaps dents — but it will take a big bang to crack it or to spring a rivet.

Aluminum is also immune to weather. It will not rot or mildew. A hot sun may make it warm to the touch, but it will not crack the finish. It will not rust, even in salt water. All this means that an aluminum canoe is almost maintenance free, which is why they have become so popular with canoe liveries and canoeing outfitters. After all, these people do not have time to do heavy maintenance. Also, they do a lot of business with tyro canoeists who are frequently hard on canoes. It is for these same reasons that aluminum canoes have become almost the official craft of Boy Scout troops over much of the United States and Canada.

Aluminum is very buoyant and rides high. This can be a curse in a heavy headwind, but at any other time no canoe responds with the same ease as aluminum. You can turn it with three paddle strokes. It pivots on a spot.

The modern aluminum canoe has other virtues. With air flotation chambers, it is virtually unsinkable. Even when upset, it will right itself automatically. However, this can be a double-edged sword. It's generally a good feature to have, but if there is a strong wind the canoe can be blown out of reach much faster than a man can swim.

The aluminum canoe is not without its faults. For example, it is difficult to pole because its light, buoyant bow is easily turned by even light winds and current. It is hot on a sunny day and, if you kneel in it right after ice-out, the cold comes right up and chills you to the marrow. But, perhaps worst of all, is the fact that aluminum is noisy. Every scrape and rub can be heard a long way off. Even tiny wavelets bouncing off the gunwales can sound like tin drums. Aluminum canoes are poor hunting craft for deer or moose.

Many people object to the color of raw aluminum. This, of course, is no real problem because you can paint it any color

36

you wish. Grumman, the largest manufacturer of canoes, sells canoes that are painted in many bright colors, and even one in a "dead grass" color for duck hunters. Of course, once an aluminum canoe is painted, it is no longer maintenance free.

Despite its ruggedness, the aluminum canoe is not indestructible. Smash into a rock hard enough and it will crack. We have also seen them badly battered in rapids. An experienced canoeist still exhibits care and caution with his craft, even if it is aluminum.

There are a number of specialized aluminum canoes on the market aimed at the "non-canoeist." The Sportspal is perhaps the best known of these. This is a short, wide canoe made of extra-thin aircraft aluminum. Because of its great width, it is extremely stable but difficult to handle in rough water or in the wind. In fact, it can be rowed more easily than paddled.

This type of canoe, however, does have its uses. Because they are lined with a foam rubber type of material which deadens sound, they are fairly quiet. They are good craft for the angler on small, quiet brooks and small lakes. We use one for duck hunting on small marshes and beaver ponds. A retriever can easily leap from it without risk of tipping.

Synthetics. Synthetics have become *the* canoe-building material. They come close to being ideal for mass manufacture. As a result, there is a profusion of synthetic canoes on the market, made of fiberglass, ABS plastic, and other materials. In the early years of the fiberglass canoe, many poorly designed models were made; this is no longer true. Makers like Old Town and Sawyer have designed and made outstanding synthetic canoes.

The best racing canoes today are made of synthetics, as are the voyageur-type which accommodates a dozen paddlers with ease. Fiberglass canoes today outsell all others, partly because they are cheaper than aluminum. In fact, we sometimes wonder how some of the department and discount sporting goods stores can sell them for so little. There is no doubt that synthetic canoes are the best buy for the budget-conscious canoeist.

Fiberglass is as maintenance-free as aluminum. It is cooler in summer and warmer in cold water than aluminum, and as durable. Fiberglass too, can be dragged over gravel bars and beaver dams. But again, this does not mean that they are indestructible. They can be punctured and they can crack. Another worthwhile feature of fiberglass canoes is that their colors are built right in, so they never fade.

Synthetic canoes also have their faults. Drag one over too many beaver dams and rocky shoals and you can bet the laminates will start to wear away. Conventional fiberglass is also very heavy. For this reason, fiberglass canoes are not the ideal craft for canoe tripping where there are many portages to conquer. However, this is not true for some of the other synthetics. For example, the Abitibi canoe, made by the Pine Tree Canoe Company is manufactured by laminating a synthetic material called Kelvar 49 between wire mesh. Kelvar is 60 percent lighter than fiberglass and supposedly even more durable. A 16-foot Abitibi weighs a mere 34 pounds.

The only way a fiberglass canoe can be made unsinkable is to build in flotation material. The Old Town Canoe Company has done this with some of its canoes by layering vinyl, ABS plastic, and foam. A 17-foot Chipewyan Tripper 37 inches wide and 15 inches deep weighs only 74 pounds.

Before closing this section on synthetically covered canoes, we would be remiss if we did not mention that there are several fiberglass canoe kits on the market for the do-it-yourselfer.

Try a Test Run

There is really only one way to find out how a canoe feels and handles, and that is to get in and paddle it. Unfortunately this is not always possible. Not all marinas and canoe dealers are on water. And even those that are may not be happy about putting a new canoe into the water for you to try out.

However, there are canoe dealers who keep demonstrators around for that purpose. Another way to try out a canoe is to go to a canoe livery and rent each of the various types. You may find one that you like.

If a test run is out of the question, look over as many canoes as you can and keep in mind the roles that the keel, the flat or round bottom, and the width play in the performance of a canoe.

CHAPTER 4

On Paddles and Paraphernalia

Next to a canoe, a paddle is the most important piece of equipment that a canoeist owns. Paddles are not the only gear; life jackets, ropes, anchors, safety helmets, pontoons and outriggers, carrying yokes, and cartop carriers are other essentials.

Choosing a Paddle

The rule of thumb is that a paddle should come to the chin of the bowman and to the eyes of the sternman. This rule is reasonably accurate. Novice paddlers could do worse than to adopt it, at least until they gain experience and can decide whether they prefer paddles that are a shade shorter or longer. Seasoned canoeists usually prefer paddles that are a bit longer. A long shaft makes for better leverage, and gives longer reach for good sweeps, but the crucial factor is that the entire blade be in the water when paddling, not just two-thirds of it.

If you intend to paddle a canoe from a standing position, you will need a paddle that is longer than normal. Here, a good rule of thumb is to get one two or three inches longer than your height.

However, in our opinion, the most important rule to follow when choosing a paddle is one which we are about to coin — the paddle must feel comfortable. It must be almost an extension of yourself. To accomplish this, more than paddle length must be considered — the type of grip, blade length, and blade width all have a bearing on how it feels and handles.

39

The Grip

The grip determines how comfortably it fits into the paddler's hand, or, perhaps more correctly, how comfortably the paddler's hand fits over the grip. Remember, there is a strong correlation between efficiency and comfort. Essentially there are three types of grips: the pear, the flaring, and the T. The so-called pear grip is the most widely used. As the name suggests, the tip has a rounded, pear shape, which allows for a firm, comfortable hold from all angles.

The flaring shape is similar to the pear grip, but is wider and more flared at the top. It is a bigger, more hand-filling grip, and hence is frequently preferred by men with large hands.

The T grip, as the name suggests, is T-shaped. It is generally thought of as a racing paddle grip, and allows a firm grasp on the paddle.

Then there is the paddle which has no real grip at all. It simply ends like a broom handle, but gripless paddles are rarely encountered today. Western Indians used them many years ago.

Blade Length

Blade length is another consideration. To a large degree, the length of the blade is predetermined by the overall length of the paddle. Generally, blade lengths range from 26 to 30 inches.

Blade Width

More important is blade width. Modern canoe paddles range from 6 to 10 inches in width. All widths have their advantages and disadvantages. The wider the blade, the more tiring the paddle is to use. The narrower the blade, the more strokes you have to make and the longer it takes to get anywhere. The same claims can also be made for blade length. After all, it is both length and width that determine the surface area of the paddle.

It requires less energy to draw a narrow blade through the water because its bearing surface has a smaller area. On the other hand, more strokes are required with a narrow paddle. It is easier to wield, particularly for youngsters and women. A

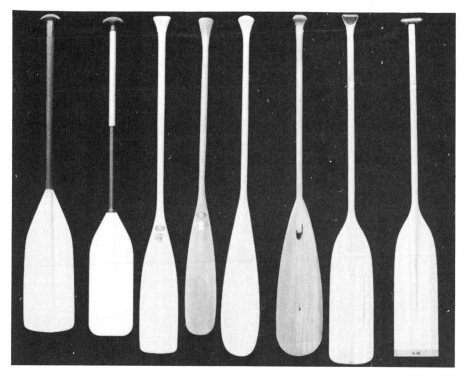

Canoe paddles come in a variety of blade widths and grip styles. A wide blade has more thrust, but a narrow one requires less energy to draw through water.

wide blade produces more thrust and is more tiring, but it will propel a canoe faster and will make it respond faster if you have to pivot around rocks or deadheads.

We prefer wider blades, but we realize that wider blades are not a good choice for everyone. A canoeist who wants to use a wide-bladed paddle should be in good physical shape. The secret to paddling with wide blades is to take a tiny rest between strokes.

For what it's worth, we have noticed a geographic trend in widths of canoe blades. Easterners prefer wider blades than canoeists from the mid-west and Great Lakes areas. We do not know why, but it could stem back to the Indian days. The Ojibways, Fox, and Crees used narrower paddles than the eastern tribes such as the Micmacs and Possamaquaddies.

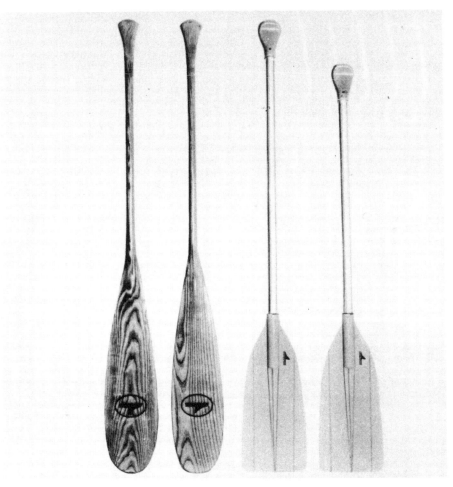

Wood is still the most popular material for paddle construction; however, many white water canoeists prefer paddles of plastic with aluminum shafts.

We recommend blades of about 6 inches in width for youngsters and women. For seasoned paddlers, a width of 7 to 7½ inches is a better bet.

Blade Shapes

There are three basic blade shapes: the *square-off* which is preferred by canoe racers, the *beaver-tail,* and the *Maine guide.*

From these three basic shapes have sprung a number of variations.

The square-off is well suited for the fast, chopping stroke of a canoe racer, and is good for fast water. It has a wide blade; the shape comes from the Crees who made similar but narrower paddles.

We are very fond of the Maine guide blade shape. It is a classic, with slim lines, very utilitarian. Why this paddle is called Maine guide we do not know, because it shows a definite Ojibway influence. Ojibway country is a long way from the state of Maine.

The beaver-tail blade is probably a spin-off from the Maine guide. It is not as slim or as attractive, but still very serviceable.

Paddle Construction

Paddle construction — material and method — is another important factor. Ash is the most commonly used wood. It is tough, durable, extremely hard, and quite limber, an important asset for a canoe paddle. Sugar maple is another frequently used wood. It is hard and durable, even more so than ash, but heavier. The same goes for black cherry which, for this reason, is less popular.

There are also paddles made of spruce. They are light, but very brittle. For this reason, we believe that they should never be taken on wilderness canoe trips, unless you take along a couple of spares. The biggest virtue of spruce paddles is their light weight, hence they are frequently chosen for women and children. This is fine for paddling around the camp or cottage, but not for paddling in the wilderness. Another reason for the popularity of spruce is its low cost. Again, one must realize that low cost does not always mean money saved. A paddle that snaps in its first season is hardly a good investment.

A canoeist who wants a light but still durable paddle should look at the laminates made from Sitka spruce and hardwood inserts. They are quite strong, certainly strong enough not to snap, even with rugged use, in a race. They are, though, somewhat expensive.

The problem with the laminates is that there are so many on the market that are of poor quality and construction. It is difficult for a novice to tell the good from the bad. The best advice we can give is to select paddles made by well-known canoe makers. No manufacturer of a well-made canoe will equip it with an inferior paddle.

Because of the relatively recent interest in white-water canoeing and kayak racing, aluminum and high-strength plastic paddles are now available. The shaft is generally a hollow aluminum tube, while the blade and grip are made of fiberglass. These paddles are very light and strong, but expensive.

Choosing a paddle is not easy. Once you have decided on length, grip type, and blade width, look at the construction. There should be no rough edges on the grip and no rough spots on the shaft, which invariably cause blisters. Be leery of paddles that are painted or covered with too much varnish. The paint and varnish might be covering up something. Check for knots and other defects, especially on the shaft. Observe the grain of the wood. It should always run lengthways: straight down the paddle. Sight down the paddle for straightness. Maple and ash paddles warp if improperly stored.

The blades on quality paddles should be feathered along the edges and bottom so that the edges are of uniform thickness. Many high-quality paddles also have fiberglass-coated blades to prevent wear.

Other Canoeing Paraphernalia

A canoeist needs more than a canoe and a paddle to indulge in his sport safely and efficiently. Let us consider safety first. Every canoeist should own a good life preserver and should get into the habit of wearing it, at least on big lakes and turbulent rivers. There are a number of good, government-approved life preservers that are not at all bulky and the new flotation windbreakers and jackets are also a good bet in the fall and spring when the weather is cool.

No one should run white water without wearing a crash helmet. Without one, head injuries are a real risk. (Crash helmets and life preservers are both available from marinas and canoe and kayak dealers.)

There is a whole array of canoeing accessories such as masts for sails, brackets for motors, and pontoons for extra stability.

A rope is a handy piece of equipment. It is a must for tracking. Also, there are times when a canoe cannot be beached easily, so the only way to secure it is with a rope. Whether to choose a rope of synthetic or natural fibers is always a dilemma. Both have their advantages. Nylon ropes float and, because they are brightly colored, are not as easily lost or misplaced. They are cheaper and will not rot. But they burn the skin more readily if they slide through your hand. Ropes made from natural fibers are smoother and not likely to burn as much. However, they are more expensive and will rot if left outside over winter.

Our preference: nylon ropes for anchor lines and natural ropes for tracking lines. What length and thickness? Thirty to 40 feet of ⅜ inch rope is ample.

Most canoeists never need an anchor, and if they do they can improvise one from a big rock. But anyone who contemplates

Cartop canoe carriers come in a variety of styles and materials for cars with or without rain gutters.

fishing or duck hunting over decoys will need one. A number of good, light anchors are available, made principally for small, cartop boats. These are ideal for light crafts such as canoes. Many fold down when not in use. For example, Grumman makes such an anchor.

Almost every canoeist requires some sort of car roof rack or roof carrier to transport his canoe. (Canoe clubs who take part in regattas frequently have trailers which can haul several canoes at a time.) All marinas stock cartop carriers for small

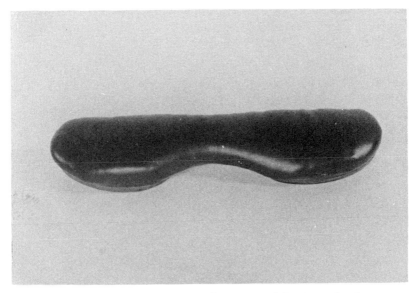

Padded portage pads or carrying yokes are useful accessories for anyone who is going to do much canoe tripping.

boats, which are generally suitable for canoes. Some of the major canoe manufacturers, such as Old Town and Grumman make them. There is even one cartop carrier made of synthetic foam that needs no bolting or clamping to the car. The tension is applied when the canoe is tied down. Shock-cord tiedowns are another good bet for lashing canoes down, but any type of rope is good. (Here is another use for your rope.)

Canoes without carrying yokes can be outfitted with optional carrying yokes bolted to the craft. Some types are detachable. There are also padded portage pads that can be bolted to the center thwart. A portaging yoke or portaging pads are useful accessories for anyone who is going to do a lot of canoe tripping.

One of the most useful bits of paraphernalia for a canoeist is a kneeling pad of sponge rubber similar to those used by charwomen. A small, inflatable air pillow also makes a fine kneeling pad. Almost every canoeist kneels to paddle at one time or another, either simply to change positions or, to keep a lower center of gravity in fast water or on rough seas. A kneeling pad becomes doubly useful when the water or weather is rough, and there is apt to be much rubbing and chafing. It is also a must in aluminum canoes in cold water. The cold comes right through the thin sheet of metal if there is no kneeling pad. And, of course, a kneeling pad is even more important if the canoeist is wearing hiking shorts. Bare knees on a canoe bottom are unpleasant.

Some canoeists who prefer to paddle in a kneeling position have even gone as far as to have pads fitted for their knees, in much the same way as soccer goalkeepers' knee pads. Canoe Imports of Burlington, Vermont, market commercially made kneeling pads that strap around the knees. And, of course, you can always improvise a kneeling pad from a jacket or other garment.

Also available are splash covers, seat cushions, floor seats for passengers, and underseat gear bags. Only you can tell how useful or necessary such accessories are for you. Most are made by the bigger canoe manufacturers, specifically for their craft, but some suit any type of canoe.

Then there are keels, pontoons, rudders, masts, sails, as well as outboard-motor side brackets for canoeists who want to sail or power their canoes. We will have more to say about these in later chapters.

PART II
Wetting a Paddle

The Colorado River is famous for its white water and magnificent scenery. Note the boarding procedure.

50

CHAPTER 5

Getting into a Canoe

Canoes are quite often upset even before the paddles are wetted. Undeniably, getting into a canoe or out of it requires care, vigilance, and experience. Therefore it is a good idea to practice before taking out a new canoe. Not all canoes feel the same when you first step into them. A 22-foot Hudson Bay freighter will obviously feel more stable than a 12-foot trapper's model. Similarly, a 16-foot aluminum canoe feels different from a Peovier canvas-covered cedar strip.

Make all movements slow and deliberate; the only exception would be in a canoe race, and that is an entirely different kettle of fish chowder.

Launching your canoe from a beach or a firm shoreline is fairly easy. All it takes is a normal sense of balance and a little practice. If you are doing it for the first time or trying out a new canoe, select quiet waters. A slow-moving stream or a sheltered bay are ideal.

Boarding Alone

Most lone canoeists prefer to paddle from the opposite end; that is, facing the stern and either sitting on or kneeling from the bow seat. If you have no gear or duffle, put some ballast in the bottom. A good place for ballast is usually just in front of the opposite seat in the middle of the canoe. A flat rock, a bag of sand, or any other object which weighs from 20 to 30 pounds and which will not roll or shift can be used. Avoid sharp objects that might puncture your canoe. Ballast should give the canoe stability, help hold the bow in the water, make the craft easier to steer, and improve overall maneuverability.

A bailing can and a spare life preserver may be tucked under the bow, just in case.

The very first exercise before getting into your canoe is to put on your government-approved life preserver. Consider the life preserver an essential piece of canoeing equipment. (We have more to say about life preservers and life-saving practices in Chapter 14.)

Next, position the canoe about one third in the water, with the other two-thirds resting on the beach. (Note that the stern should be in the water if you are alone and paddling from the bow as mentioned previously.) If you have ballast, check to make sure that it is exactly in the middle and not off to one side. Put the spare paddle flat on the floor with the handle facing towards shore. It should be close enough so you can reach it without having to move from your paddling position. Spare paddles lying on thwarts, across gunwales, or otherwise sticking up in the air have a habit of getting in the way or falling overboard.

Next, using both hands, lift the canoe, high enough so that the front is floating, and gently slip it into the water. Do not let go of it, but observe how it floats. Both gunwales should be parallel to the water, and the front end (in this case the stern because you are alone) should be considerably lower in the water than the bow that you are holding. At this stage some adjustment of the ballast may be necessary to put the canoe on an even keel. Now, pull the canoe back towards shore until it is just resting on it. Let go of the canoe and pick up your paddle. Hold it firmly in your right hand if getting in from the right side, in your left hand if boarding from the left.

Now, stand beside the seat that you are going to paddle from and push the paddle straight down into the water. The motion should be fairly straight up and down, made about 4 or 5 inches away from the canoe. Make sure the paddle is firmly pressed into the sand or mud, but not so far in as to make it difficult to pull out. Whether you grasp the paddle on the top or somewhere along the shaft, will depend upon your height, balance, and individual preference. Using the paddle as a staff or a prop, gently put the opposite leg into the exact middle of the canoe a few inches in front of the seat. Still using the paddle as a staff or prop, shift your weight to the leg in the canoe and ease yourself onto the seat. Now, relax a moment. This will give you a chance to see how it feels. Then, kneel down and see how that feels. Decide whether you want to paddle from the seat or kneeling on the floor.

To paddle from the kneeling position, bring the paddle into the canoe and place it with the blade away from you, either leaning against the thwart or on the bottom. Grasp the gunwales (one in each hand) and put one foot under the seat with the knee resting on the floor. Repeat with the other leg. Spread your knees slightly until you feel comfortable and well balanced. When paddling from this position, your buttocks should be pressed against the seat, or the thwart, if your canoe has no seats.

With one end of the canoe still resting on shore, you may wish to practice changing from the kneeling to the sitting position. It is easy. Just remember to shift one leg at a time while balancing yourself with the gunwales.

To launch the canoe, grasp the paddle in both hands. One hand should be around the top of the end knob, the other should be part way down the shaft. With both hands on the paddle, position the blade directly behind you and in line for a direct push. Avoid pushing sideways or up and down to get the canoe floating. Lean forward a little to put more weight forward. Keep both hands and the paddle in line with the canoe and, with the knob of the paddle as close to the water as is practical, gently push the canoe free. Care must be taken to feel with the paddle; make sure it does not slip before applying pressure to push off. The method just described is one of the safest and easiest ways to launch a canoe when you are alone. All it requires is confidence in your ability to balance yourself as you and the canoe move forward. When using this boarding technique, it is important to step right into the middle of the canoe and to keep your movements smooth and rhythmical.

Launching from a rocky shoreline requires a different technique than launching from a beach or mud bank. Here the canoe must be pushed off with a foot instead of the paddle. Simply put one foot in the exact middle of the canoe just in front of your paddling place. At the same time lean slightly forward and grasp the gunwales firmly, one in each hand. Now, push the canoe away from the shore with the other foot and ease yourself into your favorite paddling position.

Boarding from a dock is accomplished in much the same way as getting in from the shore, except that you do not have to shove off after you have boarded. Leave the canoe tied amidship so the rope will be easy to reach when you want to untie it. This is particularly important if the wind is strong and there is a chop or swell. Other than that, simply put one foot exactly in the middle of the canoe just ahead of your paddling position and, using the paddle for balance, ease yourself down into the canoe. Wait until you are settled to untie the canoe and begin paddling. Launching a canoe in busy marinas, boat-launching ramps, and recreation areas requires common sense. Avoid shoving off in front of powerboats, water skiers, or trolling fishermen. Always be on the defensive when confronted by motor-driven boats.

Getting into your canoe in fast-flowing streams or rivers is quite different from launching in quiet waters. Whether heading upstream or downstream, canoes should always be launched as parallel to the bank as possible. The only exceptions are areas around rocks, blow-downs, shallow water, or other obstacles.

To shove off, line up the canoe parallel to the shore. Then place your paddle within easy reach. Make sure your rear foot is on solid ground so it will not slip. Next, with one hand on the gunwale, lean down and put one foot exactly in the middle of the canoe just ahead of where you intend to paddle. Then, reach over and grip the opposite gunwale with the other hand. Now, remove the other foot from shore, shoving off with it, and, with one fluid motion, ease yourself down into the paddling position. Try to avoid pushing the canoe sideways as you lift your foot off shore. Always remember to keep your weight low and, at all costs, avoid jerky movements.

If it looks as though the canoe might drift into some hazard just after launching, it might be wise to transport or trail it up

54

or downstream and put it in at a safer place. Avoid launching into flowing waters above waterfalls, open dams, hydro intakes, log flumes, and other dangerous places. Make absolutely sure that you are well away from any chance of trouble.

With Two Paddlers

Getting into a canoe when there are two paddlers involved is a little easier than with one. But carelessness or a failure to communicate your intentions to the other paddler occasionally leads to problems. Therefore, it is wise to have an understanding with your partner right from the start. Talk things over, arrange for signals, and reach an agreement on the responsibilities of each paddler.

Remember, both paddlers must work as a team. This is the essence of canoeing. Teamwork must begin the moment the canoe is being boarded. Paddlers should board the canoe one at a time with one steadying the craft for the other. They can board together only if the canoe is tied to a dock at both bow and stern or if it is being held by someone else, or, if the canoe is firmly lodged in cattails or some other vegetation. But whenever simultaneous boarding is attempted, the canoeists must be familiar with each other's moves, and must exercise reasonable care and balance. We feel that simultaneous boarding is not for tyros. After you have upset and dumped most of your camping gear into 10 fathoms of water, it is too late to say "I thought *you* were going to steady the canoe!"

First decide who is going to paddle in the bow and who will paddle from the stern. Usually the heavier person will paddle in the stern. Why? Because trying to steer a bow-heavy canoe is very difficult, and if you hit any kind of swell or choppy water, it could be dangerous. Break this rule only when the more experienced canoeist is lighter than his partner. Then the extra weight in the bow must be compensated for by putting some ballast, part of the equipment load, or even rocks or a sand bag towards the stern. Use as much ballast as necessary, so that the bow of the canoe is just slightly higher than the stern when you are both in it. This gives the canoe more stability and puts it on an even keel.

Canoeing requires teamwork, even when just boarding the craft. The stern paddler stabilizes the canoe for the bowman to enter.

Launching a canoe from a sandy beach or in quiet waters is fairly straightforward. Place the canoe, with the bow pointing straight out from shore, on the water until it is free-floating. Then ease it back until the stern is touching or resting on shore. The stern paddler now places his paddle across the canoe and straddles the canoe and leans forward. His hands should be on the opposite gunwales. Either by sitting on the stern or simply applying weight downwards with both hands, it is fairly easy to stabilize the canoe and keep it from wobbling. The bowman can, by using the paddle for a staff or balance pole, now walk from the stern to the bow in reasonable safety. Some paddlers prefer to crouch down as they take their position on the front seat. In any event, keep each step slow, deliberate, and exactly in the

Paddlers should board a canoe one at a time, with one person steadying the craft for the other.

middle of the canoe. A good sense of balance is a great asset.

Once the bowman is in paddling position, he must steady the canoe for the sternman. If the water is shallow, he should use his paddle as a pole, pressing hard against the river bottom. In deep water the bowman simply holds his paddle in paddling position.

The sternman then relaxes his hold on the stern, reaches over, grabs hold of the opposite gunwale, and takes his position, almost in one fluid motion. In very shallow water it may be necessary for the sternman to ease or push the canoe out a bit as it may not float once the sternman gets in and has taken his position. It is the sternman's job to estimate how far he has to push the canoe to make it float free.

Three or More Paddlers

The boarding procedure for three or more paddlers is much the same as for two. The canoe is positioned in the water with the bow facing away from the shore. The stern is either resting on, or just free, of the shore. As with two, the sternman holds the canoe with both hands at the stern. The bowman is first to enter and proceeds to make his way to the bow seat by stepping exactly in the middle of the canoe, using his paddle for balance. Similarly, the centreman takes his position in the centre of the canoe. He faces the bow and sits flat on the floor with legs stretched forward. A blanket or a foam pad makes the floor more comfortable.

However, comfort should never override stability or safety. If lower gravity is needed for more stability, then the centreman may have to sit on the floor. Paddling from the centre position is never as much fun as from the bow seat or stern, so, if you are on a long trip, take pity on the paddler who is stuck in the middle and change positions occasionally.

If there are four paddlers, follow the same technique. The sternman holds the canoe; the bowman enters first; the second paddler takes position sitting on the bottom, back of the bowman; the third paddler takes his position back of the second. After all three are settled comfortably, the sternman eases the canoe out a little until it is free floating and then takes his position in the stern. Before boarding, the sternman may direct any of the paddlers to move a little one way or another. Some sternmen wait until they are underway to make these minor adjustments. Only the sternman can determine if the canoe is listing slightly to one side or the other. He, after all, does the steering.

With five or more paddlers, the boarding procedure is still the same. The sternman steadies the canoe and the bowman gets in first. All the other paddlers follow one at a time and take their positions from bow to stern. The key element is to board one at a time and wait until each paddler has taken his position. Generally, however, big freighter canoes are more stable because of their wide beam, length, freeboard, and weight; getting in or out is fairly easy under most conditions. It would take a team of clumsy oafs to upset a freighter.

CHAPTER 6

Getting Out of a Canoe

Canoes are just as easily upset when getting out as they are getting in. Perhaps even more so if the paddler is in a hurry, or tries to carry too much cargo, or is careless and ignores common safety precautions. Getting out requires slow, deliberate, and well-coordinated movements. Basically the procedure is the same as getting in, only the steps are reversed.

If You Are Alone

First, beach your canoe in shallow, quiet waters. To do this, lean back slightly and paddle very slowly, straight onto the beach. By leaning back just a trifle you raise the bow a little, so that when leaning forward ready to embark, the bow will be resting on the beach. This adds a little more stability and is better than paddling fast and forcing the canoe up onto the beach, perhaps scratching it or, worse, puncturing it. After the craft comes to rest, balance the paddle straight up and down alongside the canoe and ease yourself into a standing position. Now, using the paddle as a balance pole, step directly into the middle of the canoe and walk slowly to the opposite end. The canoe should become more stable as you get closer to shore. Most paddlers place a hand on the bow, or on one of the gunwales just ahead of the bow seat to steady the canoe as they step out of it. This ensures that the canoe will not slip back into the water, or, if there is a backwash or waves, that the canoe will not pound or bounce on any sharp objects.

Whenever launching or landing look the area over closely, both the shore and the shallows. Bush pilots who fly float planes and land on many lakes and rivers always circle several times and check for floating logs, sunken stumps, or other hazards before landing. They do this even if they are returning to the spot they left an hour or two ago, as half-submerged logs can always drift in. Canoeists should follow the same procedure.

Once you have landed, lay your paddle down well back from the water and lift the canoe up onto the beach. Always pull the canoe out of the water immediately. It is a horrible feeling to go ashore and build a fire, or walk around to get the kinks out, then look back only to find your canoe floating down the river. In wilderness areas it could be tragic. And it is always embarrassing, so we will stress it again. After you have landed, either tie your canoe securely to some solid object or take it completely out of the water, well up on shore.

With Two Paddlers

Landing a canoe with two paddlers is as simple as launching with two. Good communications are most important. Talk to each other. Make sure you both know exactly where you will land. Any disagreements should be settled on shore after you have landed.

On a sandy beach land straight on, if possible. Avoid broadside or trough landings if there are waves or winds. Landing along rivers and streams, especially where there is a fair bit of current, is different and we will deal with it a little later.

Never try to drive the canoe up onto the beach. Two paddlers going full out can generate considerable thrust. There is nothing wrong with paddling fast in open water, but when landing, take it easy. After you have decided on the landing site, ease up. Canoes, with a bit of weight and momentum, will coast a long way.

When coasting in for a landing, the bowman should position his paddle so that the tip or one corner of the blade is in the water exactly in line with the direction the canoe is traveling. The sternman's paddle should be dug in the water for maximum

On getting out, the bowman should hold the canoe steady while the sternman walks out, using his paddle as a prop to steady himself.

steerage. If the canoe is coming in towards shore too fast, both paddlers can shove their paddles straight down in the water and hold. They may also back paddle. Back paddling, however, takes practice.

The bowman should make sure that the canoe does not strike the beach too hard by digging the paddle into the sand or shoreline with both hands, providing, of course, the canoe is not moving too fast. Care must be taken to keep the blade of the paddle away from the bow, and not allow it to swing under the canoe. When the canoe nudges the shore, the stern paddler presses his paddle straight down into the water with both hands. If the water is too deep for this, put the paddle at a 45-degree angle, with the edge of the blade pointing towards shore. Apply

61

slight downward pressure. The paddle then acts in much the same way as an outrigger on the dugout canoes of the South Sea Islands.

After the canoe has touched shore and the sternman has stabilized it, the bowman, using his paddle as a staff, eases himself up to a standing position and steps out on shore. To prevent the bow from rising up in the air (if the canoe is loaded stern-heavy), the bowman should get out in a crouched position, keeping one hand pressed down on the gunwale to prevent the canoe from bouncing up. As soon as the bowman is out, he should lift and pull the canoe on shore a foot or two, straddle the bow, and press down hard on the gunwales. The sternman can now, using the paddle as a prop, exit from the fairly stable canoe, with every step as near the middle of the canoe as possible.

As soon as both paddlers have alighted, the canoe should be lifted — not dragged — further up on shore before unloading. Quite often canoes are upset when the sternman tries to take gear with him while leaving the canoe, invariably some valuable item like a camera, fishing rod, or rifle. So get into the habit of doing one thing at a time. First, land easy; second, have the sternman stabilize the canoe; third, have the bowman get out and hold the canoe firmly; fourth, have the sternman leave the canoe. Only after the canoe has been lifted a little further up on shore, is it ready for unloading. Secure the canoe after you have unloaded it.

This reminds us of two experienced canoeists, fishing for brook trout in a Canadian wilderness lake, when one of them caught a real "lunker." The fish may well have weighed over 12 pounds. Unfortunately, we will never know how big it was. Right after it was caught, they paddled hastily back to camp. The bowman jumped out, pulled the canoe up a bit, and headed for camp to spread the news. The sternman grabbed his camera, fishing rod, and trout, and followed him. Splash! Everything, including the fisherman went overboard. The trout, for all we know, is still swimming. But worse still, no one ever believed how "the big one got away."

Landing a canoe along rocky shorelines, stump-infested bays, or boggy marshes requires more vigilance. Both paddlers, especially the bowman, should be on the alert for sunken objects. The secret is to go slowly and carefully.

Three or More Paddlers

The same procedure is followed with three or more paddlers as with two. One paddler at a time! Usually the bowman gets out first, holds the canoe for the next paddler, and so on, until all are out, unloading only after everyone is out and the canoe is secured.

In Fast Current

Getting out of a canoe along streams or river banks, particularly in a strong current requires more finesse and experience. Landings can still be easy if you go slowly, deliberately, and one at a time. (On lakes the canoe is generally secured after unloading; on rivers it should be secured before it is unloaded.) After you have decided where to land, bring the canoe in parallel to the shore, facing upstream if possible. (Of course, this is not always possible, especially if you are going downstream and approaching a portage around a waterfall or other obstruction.) The procedure for getting out is much the same as when the canoe is beached, except that the bowman, who exits first, merely steps out on shore, preferably in a crouching position. He then holds the canoe for the sternman. If the current is really strong, tie the bow first to a tree, log, or stump to keep it from drifting, although even on very fast rivers there are usually eddies and stretches of quiet water where landings can be made.

Also, do not hesitate to take advantage of existing vegetation. Push under tag alders or willows, hang on to small branches and roots to stabilize the canoe, pull up on cattails and other densely growing marsh plants, or slip in the lee of a stump or a log.

When landing above waterfalls or other hazards, the bowman should always get on shore with the rope in hand. He can either tie the canoe or, if that is not possible, hold it steady until the sternman has got out. Occasionally it might be easier for the sternman to get out first, in which case he follows the same procedure as the bowman. Here is the proper procedure to follow when getting out of a canoe along a fast-flowing river or stream:

(1) decide on a good landing spot

(2) be careful not to run the canoe up onto logs, rocks, or other objects

(3) take advantage of existing conditions such as back eddies, logs, stumps, and even live vegetation

(4) bring the canoe parallel to the shore if possible, preferably with the bow pointing upstream

(5) one paddler, usually the bowman, gets out first and holds the canoe for the other one

(6) if necessary, tie the bowline to some object immediately after the first person gets out

(7) always secure the canoe before leaving it to look for campsites, portages, or before unloading the craft

(8) never venture too close to waterfalls, open dams, or unfamiliar rapids.

CHAPTER 7

Paddling a Canoe

Paddling a canoe — the actual learning and mastering of the different strokes — is easy. To many people it comes almost naturally. Paddling with efficiency and economy of effort only comes with practice but almost anyone can become a proficient enough paddler to undertake canoe trips; to make voyages of adventure, tranquility, and excitement that make every paddle stroke worth the effort.

Paddling Techniques

Experienced canoe trippers can paddle all day long and never get really tired. So can you, once you have mastered a few basic strokes. All it takes is a bit of practice and desire. You may even learn that it is fun.

The first step after boarding a canoe, before you even attempt your first stroke, is to get into a comfortable position. Take a few deep breaths, slouch your shoulders, move the arms, bend the upper torso from side to side, and observe how your canoe behaves on the water. If paddling alone for the first time, practice close to shore in a quiet bay or stream, and always wear a life preserver.

You cannot be comfortable or relaxed sitting up straight as a board, tense, and uptight. So relax a bit, even slouch. We recommend paddling from a kneeling position (to start with), with the buttocks resting against the seat. You can paddle from either the right or left side, depending on which feels more comfortable and natural. For a right-handed person, this generally means the left side, and vice versa for a southpaw. However, once you have learned a particular stroke, you should switch to the other side, so that you will become competent on both sides.

The Cruising Stroke

Pick up the paddle with one hand around the knob and grip the other around the shaft, just above where the paddle begins to flare. Your grip on the paddle should be firm yet relaxed. Raise the paddle so that the blade is just out of the water (about four inches or whatever feels natural) and extend the lower arm forward. The upper arm (the one holding the knob) should be extended forward, but not too far. There should be a crook in the elbow. The upper arm will also cross over slightly, in front of your eyes. Next, dip the paddle blade into the water and pull the lower arm back. At the same time, push the upper arm forward. During this stroke the lower arm should be semi-rigid, and the upper arm bent at the elbow. This, the most common paddling stroke, will come almost naturally. You will find as you make the next stroke that your upper torso will bend forward at the beginning of the stroke and will tend to straighten at the end of it. Some canoeists refer to this as a rolling action.

It is important while learning this basic stroke to keep the paddle as vertical as possible. Paddling a canoe is different than rowing a boat, and you will get the maximum thrust if you can stroke the paddle vertically. Avoid touching the gunwale with the shaft of the paddle. Paddles that are continuously rubbing against the gunwale become frayed. Gunwales that are continuously scraped by a paddle soon splinter and become unsightly.

To paddle the canoe — to propel it forward — all you have to do is repeat this stroke. You will soon discover that your canoe does not travel in a straight line. It has a tendency to turn away from the side that you are paddling on. Don't worry about it for a while. Just relax and paddle. Take long, leisurely strokes and enjoy yourself.

You have just learned the cruising stroke. It is the basic paddling stroke used by most canoeists. After a while it will become as natural as walking. Then you will want to learn more strokes,

66

THE BOW STROKE

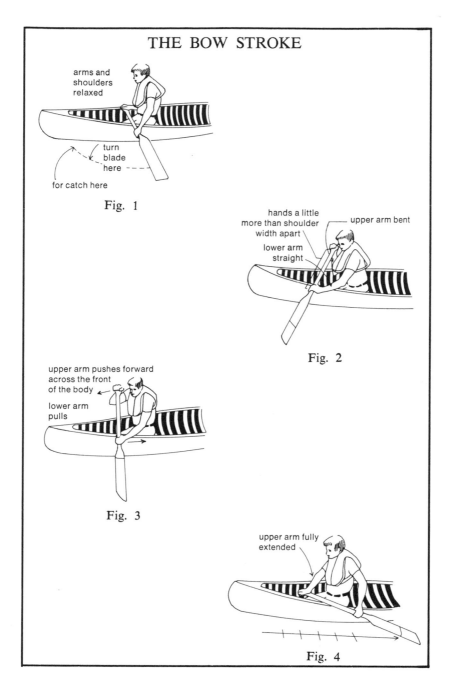

arms and
shoulders
relaxed

turn
blade
here

for catch here

Fig. 1

hands a little
more than shoulder
width apart

upper arm bent

lower arm
straight

Fig. 2

upper arm pushes forward
across the front
of the body

lower arm
pulls

Fig. 3

upper arm fully
extended

Fig. 4

The bow stroke — a cruising stroke for the paddler in the bow.

as well as how to steer the canoe, how to slow it down, and how to make it go faster. But first, perfect your cruising stroke. Become good at it! This stroke is basic to all others.

The cruising stroke is the one used by the bowman when there are two or more paddlers. It is the pace setter. It requires timing and rhythm. This short, well-timed, but deliberate stroke is best for maximum thrust with a minimum of effort. By "short" we mean a stroke that does not extend very much past the hips. There is a tendency, particularly when you are canoeing at a very leisurely pace, to allow the paddle to sweep long past the hips. There is nothing really wrong with this, but it does waste effort, energy, and time. If you are alone and responsible for both thrust and steering, you will naturally paddle past your hips to maintain steerage, so that the paddle acts almost like a rudder. But most experts agree that the short, strong stroke is easier and provides the best thrust — you go faster with less effort.

By "deliberate" we mean there should not be confusion or hesitation between strokes. Each stroke should follow the next. The movements of extending the lower arm, elbowing the upper arm, keeping the paddle vertical, and pulling through to a point just opposite the hips, should be exactly the same as in the previous stroke. But make the strokes relaxed, and above all be complete. Do not be in a hurry to go fast. One of the nice things about canoeing is that you can set whatever pace suits you.

"Well-timed" means rhythmic; that is, falling into a natural tempo. It is a mistake to paddle fast for a few strokes, then pause and paddle slowly for a while. Rather, try to find a pace that suits you and your companion, and stick to it. It is better to adopt a natural pace, even if it means paddling a little faster, and then rest and take a break every once in a while, than to set a pace that is out of time with you and your partners. Remember, canoeing means teamwork. If you are a rank novice, take it easy; a leisurely, well-timed stroke will get you there just the same.

A leisurely pace is about twenty-five to thirty strokes a minute. A fast pace, one for which you should be in good shape and fairly experienced, is between forty-five and fifty strokes a minute. Strokes of sixty or more are reserved for racers.

68

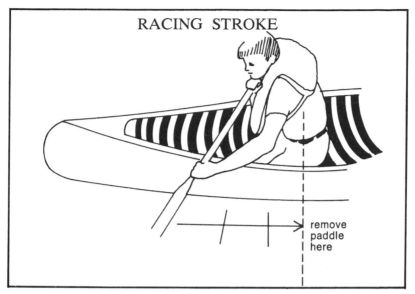

RACING STROKE

remove
paddle
here

The most remarkable feat of modern paddling combining timing, rhythm, and the short stroke with power, occurred during the summer of 1967 in northern Canada. It was during the Voyageur Canoe Pageant, an argosy of ten canoes from the ten Canadian provinces, paddling and portaging from Rocky Mountain House, Alberta, to Expo 67 in Montreal. The purpose was to commemorate the heritage of the early explorers and fur traders during Canada's centennial.

The gruelling voyage, which included forty-nine portages (one of them nine miles long) and traversed such large lakes as Winnipeg, Superior, and Huron, as well as the Ottawa and St. Lawrence Rivers, covered a distance of approximately 3400 miles and took 100 days. The route chosen retraced the path that many of the early voyageurs had paddled in their quest for furs.

The canoes weighed about 450 pounds each and were made of fiberglass. Each had a crew of six paddlers who alternated three to a side on a signal from the sternman when the canoe was underway. The canoes were required to compete against each other in lap and sprint races throughout the route. The sprints usually took place in towns and cities and were a colorful highlight of the centennial celebrations in many Canadian communities.

69

The crew from the province of Manitoba won most of the prize money for the sprints and finished with the best time. During their sprints they averaged ninety strokes per minute. Their timing and rhythm were superb; they won hands down. Each paddle went into the water at an identical angle, and at the same time. Each stroke was deliberate and short, with power.

We mention this to illustrate what can be accomplished with a canoe. After you have practiced for a while, you will find yourself falling into a natural tempo. Paddling will be the same as walking or running. Try switching sides every now and then. Avoid paddling always on the same side. Many canoeists fall into this habit unconsciously; do not become discouraged if you find it happening to you. Even the best switch hitters in baseball have a preferred side. It takes a certain amount of discipline and dedication to become a proficient paddler, so work at it. Learn to paddle from either side. You will find it extremely useful on long trips.

The Steering Strokes

There are several different names applied to the strokes used by the sternman and, at times, even the bowman, to steer a canoe. In our opinion, most of these strokes are simply variations of the same one.

The *J stroke* is the most common. The name is very apt. The stroke has a J or fish-hook shape. The paddle is stroked through the water to a point just opposite the hips of the sternman. It is then turned and pushed away from the canoe, to complete the motion that forms the letter J. This stroke produces drag, slows the canoe slightly, and tends to compensate for the torque produced by the original thrust of the paddle.

The *Canadian stroke* is similar except that, instead of pushing out the blade of the paddle, it is angled or pitched outward. Variations of the Canadian stroke consist of bringing the paddle back toward the original thrust underwater. This acts as a rudder, but produces considerable drag.

The *pitch stroke* is again similar to the Canadian but the paddle is pitched or feathered much sooner. When the paddle

70

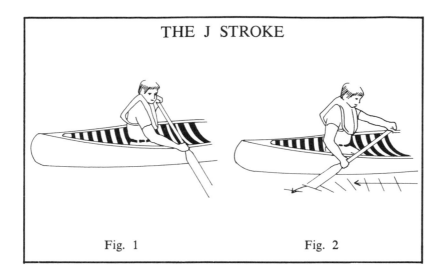

THE J STROKE

Fig. 1   Fig. 2

is about halfway through the stroke, turn it parallel to the canoe and continue through to the end of the stroke. In this way it acts more like a stern rudder. This is a smooth and easy stroke to master, does a fair job of steering, but has a couple of disadvantages: the paddle is brought out of the water while still pitched and must be reset (turned half way around) before the next stroke can begin. As a result, some forward thrust is lost, but then this is true of most steering strokes, especially when there is only one paddler.

Most of these strokes require considerable practice to master. But take lots of time. Do not try them all at once. Find out how the canoe behaves while using the cruise stroke. See how it turns when you apply the pitch stroke. Notice how, if you feather the paddle at an outward angle and pull in, the canoe turns in the direction of the pull. Observe how, when you feather the paddle at an outward angle and push gently out, it swings in the direction of your push.

There is another stroke that you can use to paddle and steer your canoe — the *Indian stroke*. It is used a lot by northern Indians and fur trappers who travel long distances during the short fall trapping season in the northern regions of Canada. Even the Eskimos of the MacKenzie Delta in the Arctic use it while paddling their large freighter canoes. This stroke consists of digging the paddle in the direction of the pull rather than straight up or down. The routine stroke is completed at this angle with little or no pitching, usually short, seldom extending beyond the hips. The beauty of it is that it does not waste time steering, as this is done while the stroke is being made. Unfortunately, it is difficult to master, and we do not recommend it until you have mastered some of the more basic paddling techniques. After that, try it. It really can move a canoe.

Another stroke, one used by hunters and wildlife photographers who have to paddle as silently as possible, is the so-called *hunter's stroke*. With this stroke the paddle blade never leaves the water. It begins with an ordinary cruise stroke, but halfway through, the paddle is turned parallel to the gunwales, circled outwards, and returned as a rudder to the forward paddle position. The paddle blade remains in the water as additional strokes are made. Depending on the type of paddle used, the blade is not plunged as deeply into the water as with ordinary paddling. This stroke can be practically soundless. Some of the experts who use it regularly actually taper both edges of the paddle blade. Paddling quietly along the shore of a remote lake on a still morning certainly has its advantages. This stroke, incidentally, is also sometimes referred to as the "Indian" stroke, because it is so quiet. However, we do not think this term is right. Indians used it only when hunting, not for general travel. It is too tiring for long-distance travel.

Back Strokes

Now that you have the canoe going ahead, you will want to be able to stop it and make it go backwards. This, too, is easy to do. All you have to do is paddle backwards. Canoes can be slowed down by merely thrusting the paddle straight down in the water and holding it there. Before attempting this, make sure you have a good hold on the paddle with both hands and that you are holding the paddle straight up and down. Be careful that the paddle blade does not twist or slip under the canoe. Practice with a slow-moving canoe before using it on an actual canoe trip.

THE BACKWATER OR BACK STROKE

Fig. 1

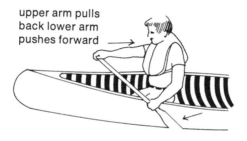

upper arm pulls
back lower arm
pushes forward

Fig. 2

Fig. 3

73

Paddling backwards requires a fair bit of coordination. Try a few strokes while the canoe is still. Get the feel of it, and notice the adjustments that have to be made, compared with going forward. At first you may find it awkward. But, it is sometimes necessary to paddle backwards, so learn how. Like all the other strokes, it will come in handy some day.

Sideway Strokes

Yes, it is really necessary to sometimes paddle sideways. There will be times when you want to slip the canoe sideways, either at one end or the entire craft. Sideway strokes are very important when traveling on fast-flowing streams or rivers. To do this, the paddle is dug into the water with the blade parallel to the gunwales. Next, you either push or pull laterally, depending on which way you want the canoe to move. It is always best to keep the keel, if the canoe has one, in line with the flow of water. Clearing rocks or other obstructions is frequently done by side strokes. The bowman or sternman pulls or pushes the canoe sideways to slip around them. Again, as with conventional paddling, the blade should be fairly vertical. A canoe can be turned right around in three or four seconds using side strokes. The draw or pull stroke is probably used more often than the push stroke, but both are effective. Practice both until you have mastered them.

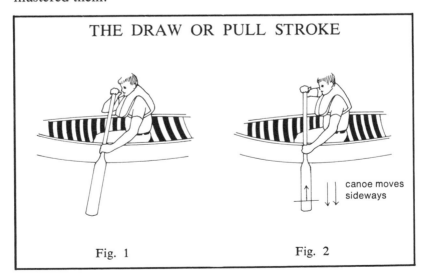

THE DRAW OR PULL STROKE

canoe moves sideways

Fig. 1   Fig. 2

74

Another version of the push stroke is the pry stroke. This consists of jamming the paddle straight down in the water parallel to the gunwale and prying out with the shaft held tightly against the gunwale. It works well if the water is deep enough. Care must be taken, though, if the blade strikes rocks or sunken logs, not to break the paddle. If you intend to canoe on fast rivers, there will be times when you will want to move the bow or stern of your canoe quickly. The pry stroke is ideal for this. Become familiar with it. Like all strokes and techniques in canoeing, all it takes is common sense and practice. You will note when you try it that the gunwale acts as a fulcrum, and that as you pry against it, the canoe is pushed downward as well as sideways. This is important to keep in mind if your canoe is loaded.

More Paddling Tips

Even after you have mastered all the strokes, there is still much to learn, especially if there are two or more paddlers in the canoe. For one thing, communicate. Talk to each other. If you want to change sides let everyone know, and agree on a time to change. As we mentioned earlier, the sternman is usually in charge, so he should call the shots.

If you are in the bow, try to set a pace that suits the other paddlers and one that all can keep up with. If there are three or more paddlers, try to synchronize your strokes. Rhythm is the secret ingredient for success.

Paddle comfortably. This is very important. If the canoe is off balance there is a natural tendency to lean the opposite way to right it. This can result in a sore back, particularly for the sternman. Shift over or move your gear. Use artificial ballast or part of your load as the ballast to balance the canoe if there is great weight disparity between paddlers.

Check your paddle from time to time. A paddle that whips in the water will soon break. And, above all, do not start out on a trip out of shape. Get some paddling in, even if it is only simulated, prior to the trip.

Paddling a canoe is good exercise. Also, it is fun. Always practice good judgment and use common sense; then you will get the most out of it.

Poling is done while standing in a canoe. It is an ideal way to propel a canoe in shallow water or in marshes and swamps where the canoeist needs to always look ahead for obstructions.

76

CHAPTER 8

With Pole and Rope

The expert polers who canoe famous salmon rivers like the Miramichi and the Restigouche in New Brunswick can actually pole upstream through rapids with one hand and roll a cigarette with the other. They also shatter the theory that no one should ever stand up in a canoe. Contrary to popular belief, canoes — the well designed ones — are not tippy or unstable. True, they are not as stable as a johnboat or a dory, but they can hold their own with most small sailboats and many shallow-draft runabouts. An experienced canoeist can easily stand and pole a canoe.

There is no doubt that poling has its place in canoeing. It is ideal for downstream travel where the water is fairly shallow — no more than a foot or so. It is excellent for marshes and swamps because it enables the canoeist to stand and look over the tops of the cattails. And, in slow-moving streams, it allows the canoeist to see over high banks.

Log drivers, like the canoeists of New Brunswick, frequently pole their riverboats on the spring log drives. They use a pike pole. A pike pole is about two inches in diameter, 10 to 12 feet long. It has a cast iron point and a spread hook flanged over the bottom end. It makes a good implement for poling. But it is a bit heavy. Its original use was for prodding and pulling logs that were stuck on something so they would be free to flow down the river, hence it was an invaluable tool in breaking up log jams. Many of today's canoe polers use fiberglass, aluminum, or bamboo poles. A straight pole of hickory or ash is also good, but you must have it shod with a bit of iron to keep the pole from fraying on the bottom. The iron or steel shoe also gets a better bite on rocks, sunken stumps, and logs. The top end of the pole can be taped or fixed with some type of knob much the same way a hockey player tapes the end of his stick. This tape or knob serves to remind you that you have reached the end of your pole, and you must either hold or reset for the next push. A poler never looks at his pole as he is poling, but always watches the water ahead. To properly pole a canoe, the canoe must be trimmed; that is, weighted correctly. Most experienced polers prefer a canoe that is weighted slightly bow-heavy — contrary to the usual stern-heavy canoe — so it will stay in line while being poled. (Putting ballast in the bow is an easy way to achieve this.)

The basic poling technique is not difficult. To begin with, stand up and balance your legs against the seat and the nearest thwart. If there is no thwart near enough, it might be easier to straddle either the rear or front seat depending on which end you are poling from. Jab the pole into the water just behind where you would normally start your paddle stroke. Grasp the pole as far down the shaft as is comfortable, and push downwards. As the canoe starts to move ahead, work your hands one over the other towards the knob at the end of the pole. When you reach the end, relax, steady the canoe, and prepare for the next thrust. Lift the pole entirely out of the water (avoid dragging it) and jab it down to get another bite. Repeat the hand maneuver to get another thrust. You are now poling. Your canoe may move a little sideways at the bow. Compensate by angling it slightly to the side from which you are poling.

If you miss a thrust, or the pole slips in fast water and the canoe starts to swing, get a solid grip on the pole, jab straight down, and hang on. Usually, if the water is deep enough and the canoe does not hang up on something, it will turn completely around. Go back down and start over. The main thing is not to panic. Keep cool, and hang in there. Try to keep the canoe in line with the current, especially the channel bends. The current in bends has a tendency to cut corners.

If both the bowman and steerman are poling, it is customary to pole on the same side. The polers then alternate. One holds while the other resets and pushes; then, as one reaches the end of his pole, he holds while the other resets and poles. By alternating, the canoe moves ahead at a steady pace and control is maintained at all times.

No one can consider himself an expert canoeist until he learns how to pole. Practice in quiet water first. Only when you have mastered the rudiments, can you tackle faster water. Poling is the fastest way of canoeing upstream in fast water that is too deep to wade out and track. Of course it is not a substitute for portaging around white water.

Tracking

When a canoeist encounters rapids, he has three options — shoot them if he has the skill and is traveling downstream, portage around them, or track them. What is tracking? It is simply floating the canoe, either up or downstream by means of a rope or pole. Tracking, or lining as it is sometimes called, can also be done if the water is too shallow to float a loaded canoe plus paddlers.

The first step is to tie a strong rope to the bow or stern, depending on whether you are going up or downstream. If you are traveling downstream, the line is tied to the stern and the canoe is floated down as you walk alongside it or on shore. It may be necessary to keep a paddle or pole handy to guide the canoe at the bow or amidship around rocks and sunken logs. When going upstream, the canoe is pulled up from a rope secured to the bow. The method is the same except that a pole or paddle is sometimes used to keep the canoe from scraping along the banks.

Tracking is a far easier task for two paddlers than one. Both can handle ropes, or, one can handle the rope while the other keeps the canoe away from banks or boulders with a paddle or pole. Canoes can be tracked either loaded or empty. With a loaded canoe, care should be taken when going over rocks or fallen logs. Heavily loaded canoes could be punctured, damaged, even broken in two.

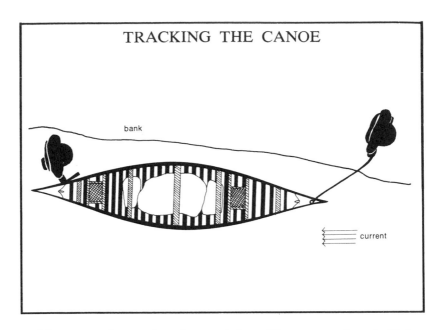

TRACKING THE CANOE

bank

current

The secret is to take plenty of time. Keep an ax handy if the going is tough among tangles of alders and willows that grow out into the water. Tracking is not difficult. If you do get bogged down, hung up on snags, or if ropes tangle, simply secure the canoe, unload, and portage.

CHAPTER 9

With Sail and Motor

Sailing a Canoe

Any canoeist who intends to do much traveling on lakes will be wise to learn how to sail a canoe. Some canoes, such as the Hudson Bay freighter, come equipped with a mast hole in the mid thwarts, but masts can be lashed to the thwart or forward seat of just about any canoe. Sailing rigs, complete with clamp-on aluminum masts, are also available. Indians along the Pacific coast of Oregon, Washington, and British Columbia were at one time quite expert at sailing their dugout canoes. The average canoe tripper does not usually bother to pack a sail and rigging along. Sailing, though, can offer a much-needed rest from the rigors of paddling on long trips. So why not learn how to rig one up?

An emergency or temporary sail can easily be made by lashing any pole 1½ to 3 inches in diameter and 8 to 12 feet in length to the forward thwart to serve as a mast. It is a good idea to secure the pole with four guy ropes to the gunwales as well. A simple square-rigger sail can be made of any light canvas. In a pinch, a piece of polyethylene sheeting, a large garbage bag, or even a large jacket or rain poncho can be used. Your paddle will serve as a tiller. Such a rig is useful only for downward sailing. There will be little or no leeway for tacking, but even so, it can give you a rest from the paddle and move the canoe at surprising speed.

We will never forget the story told to us by the captain of the *Fort Severn,* one of the Hudson Bay Company's supply ships.

81

Sailing a canoe is lots of fun, and can even be useful to canoe trippers on lake crossings. Sails and masts are available from most canoe dealers.

"We were anchored" the Captain began, "trying to ride out a three-day blow coming off the ice packs to the north. It was August, but you'd never know it by the chill. I was on the bridge checking the sky for any signs of a let up. The combers must've been running 20 feet. All at once I spotted a canoe coming down from the north. He had a poncho hoisted on about a 10-foot mast, and he was really moving. His freighter canoe was loaded to the gunwales with stove, tent, sleigh, cooking outfit, wife, kids, and at least four good-sized huskies Probably moving to another campsite further down the coast. He had an outboard motor on the stern, but he wasn't using it.

"They all smiled and waved as we watched them go by," the captain continued. "My first mate said, 'Now, there's a fellow knows what he's doing. Probably ran short of gas, waited for the

Although side brackets for outboard motors are available for double-ended canoes, anyone who contemplates using a motor a great deal should get a canoe with a V or square stern.

right wind, and is making it pay.' We watched him disappear into the twilight, and couldn't help but marvel, and wish him a safe trip."

Canoes and Outboards

An outboard motor can be used on nearly every canoe, even the lightweight 12-foot trapper's model. Motor brackets are available for all types of conventional canoes. A do-it-yourselfer can even make his own. The brackets are generally attached to the port or left side of the canoe, just behind the stern seat. They hang out over the water somewhat, and once the motor is on it makes for an unbalanced load. You have to compensate for this when loading and seating the passengers. In all cases, brackets should be securely attached to the canoe and the motor should be equipped with a safety chain. Yet the conventional double-ender was not designed for an outboard motor, and anyone contemplating using an outboard a great deal should get a square stern or a V-stern. Square or V-sterns are basically work canoes. Prospectors, surveyors, and trappers in the Canadian north use them extensively. They are also used for transporting supplies into hinterland outposts where narrow water courses and portages exclude heavier and more cumbersome boats.

Again, as with bracketed motors, it is important to match the motor to the canoe. A 25-foot Rupert's House Canoe, designed for the big waters around Hudson Bay, will accommodate an outboard motor up to 75 horsepower. This freighter canoe is so buoyant that some outboards require a longer shaft than usual. Such a canoe can easily transport a ton of supplies when properly loaded. The average 18-foot V-stern will handle an outboard motor of up to 12 horsepower, while an 18-foot square stern will take an 18-horsepower outboard motor without overpowering it. Sixteen-foot V- or square-stern canoes should not be powered with outboards of more than 7 or 8 horsepower.

Once a canoe is equipped with an outboard motor, it may come under the jurisdiction of such agencies as Harbor Commissions, Coast Guard, or Marine Authorities. This jurisdiction depends on the horsepower rating of the motor, with 10 horsepower generally being the point at which the canoe must be registered and must meet regulations in respect to life-saving equipment, fire extinguishers, and possibly other gear. In effect, the canoe then is considered a powerboat in the eyes of the law and it must meet the regulations affecting powerboats.

Operating motor-powered canoes is a different ball game from paddling. Load distribution requires reassessment. Usually more weight is needed in the bow, as the weight and power of the motor tend to lift the bow out of the water. The faster one goes, the higher the bow is lifted. This makes steering more difficult. Negotiating fast rivers, narrow channels, or shallow bays, can be hazardous if you use a motor that sheers pins. Paddles must be handy in case of emergency at all times.

84

Some disadvantages of canoeing with an outboard motor include: less carrying capacity because of the motor and gas cans; severely impaired maneuverability (fast turns are nearly impossible); and restricted use, especially in shallow waters. With gas and motor, you also have more to portage. And, of course, the craft becomes noisy and the fumes smelly. The canoe also becomes more costly to operate. We mention these angles merely to point out some of the less attractive features. Canoeing with an outboard motor does, however, have advantages. It is usually faster, less tiresome, and more practical when heavy cargoes are transported over long distances. Indeed, some freighter canoes are difficult to paddle. Canoes with outboard motors are most useful to prospectors, surveyors, trappers, and others who make their living in the bush. They are also very useful for fishing on big waters.

Our opinion of motors on double-ended canoes is mixed. The motor is an afterthought and, like most afterthoughts, it never fits well. We repeat, if you want to use an outboard motor on a canoe regularly, then get a canoe that was designed for use with an outboard motor.

In some wilderness areas the use of outboard motors is not permitted. If you plan to take a motor along on your next canoe trip, check the local regulations before you take off.

CHAPTER 10

Loading the Canoe

There is a right and a wrong way to load any boat. Even the giant freighters that ply the oceans must be loaded properly — just ask any first mate.

Canoes that are properly loaded ride better on the water, are easier to handle and maneuver, and are usually safer. Overloaded or improperly loaded canoes are difficult to steer, often uncomfortable, and downright dangerous. Resolve, therefore, from the outset never, even under the most perfect of conditions, to overload your canoe. Every canoe has a limit to the weight of the cargo it can safely transport. These recommendations are usually furnished with the canoe at the time of purchase. If not, ask for them. This information may not be available from canoe rentals, but most canoe-trip outfitters know the recommended loads and will advise you. A good rule of thumb is that a fully loaded canoe, including the paddlers, should have a minimum of six inches of freeboard amidship. That means that after the canoe is loaded and the paddlers are in place, there should be a minimum of six inches between the water and the top of the gunwales, measured at the lowest sweep of the gunwales, usually just aft of amidship.

Load in an orderly and organized manner. The first step is to have all your gear handy. Carry it down to the water's edge and pile it together. Scattered objects have a habit of getting lost. Avoid, if possible, an excessive number of loose objects. This is particularly important if there are to be many portages. So,

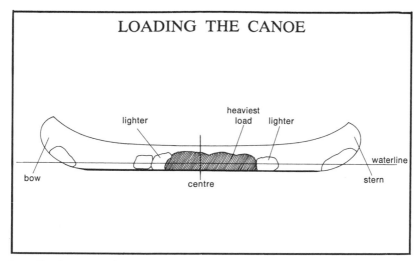

LOADING THE CANOE

lighter

heaviest
load

lighter

waterline

bow

centre

stern

bundle loose objects together or stuff them into dunnage bags. Rucksacks or packsacks are ideal. Backpacks with frames or packboards are fine for hiking, but their stiffness and bulk make them less than ideal for canoeing.

If your canoe is not equipped with splash covers, take precautions to keep sleeping bags, food, clothing, and other duffle dry. This can be done by wrapping everything in water-repellent canvas or by storing it in water-resistant containers. Even plastic garbage bags can be used, especially if they are tied securely. Maps and charts should be in clear plastic waterproof cases.

Keep in mind that the centre of gravity must be low. Begin by putting long sturdy objects (tent poles, ax) lengthwise across the ribs. They will allow for bilge water if water splashes over the gunwales. If you are expecting rain or rough water, it may even be wise to cut a few slim poles to put in the bottom of the canoe to hold the cargo up off the bottom.

Pack the heavy stuff — grub boxes, tents — amidship. Packsacks and other medium weight items should be packed towards the stern. The lightest duffle should go just back of the bow seat. Leave kneeling space for each paddler, just in case. Binoculars, cameras, fishing rods, and other fragile items should be left on top, but lashed to a thwart or seat.

If the canoe is being loaded from a beach, slip it into the water every once in a while to see how much more cargo it will hold.

After you have finished loading, ease it out into the water and rock it a few times. If anything is shifting or rolling around, re-pack it. Also, watch how the canoe rides. This will show you whether the load is properly balanced. After the first loading you will learn where each item belongs in order to get a balanced load. As a finishing touch, particularly if you anticipate rain or big waves, a ground sheet or tarpaulin should be fitted over the load and tucked in under the fore and aft thwarts. The tarp will further help to waterproof the load. You can also lash the tarp to the gunwales, seats, or thwarts. And, above all, keep a spare paddle handy in case you break or drop yours overboard in fast water.

To sum up, here are the main points to remember:

(1) do not overload — remember, six inches of freeboard
(2) keep the centre of gravity low
(3) pack heavy gear amidship
(4) make sure the load does not shift or roll
(5) lash everything down
(6) leave room to paddle from the kneeling position
(7) place maps or charts in a plastic container; keep it handy in either bow or stern
(8) keep an extra paddle handy
(9) check the shore to be certain that you have not left anything behind
(10) use good judgment and common sense at all times.

CHAPTER 11

The Portage

The canoe is really nothing more than a long, slim, portable boat. "Portable" is the important word here. It was its portability — the light weight — that made the birch-bark canoe so valuable in the exploration and fur-trade era. Canoes were the only boats light and slim enough to be carried between water courses. They made the penetration of the wilderness possible. Perhaps the most famous and historically significant portage is Grand Portage in Minnesota — eight miles of black fly and mosquito-infested lowland between the Pigeon River and Lake Superior. Now a national monument, it remains much the same as it was in the heyday of the voyageurs. Many famous explorers, missionaries, and just plain renegades have traveled across Grand Portage. It is a real challenge to any canoeist. But if you do not feel up to it, take heart. It caused La Verendrye's men to mutiny when they first tackled it in 1731. But Grand Portage was something more than just a portage. It was a meeting place, where 1200 or more voyageurs met each summer to exchange furs and skins from the northwest for trade goods and rum from Montreal. It was the boundary between the east and the west. But enough of the glamour and romance of portaging. Let's get to the serious business of actually doing it.

There is one cardinal rule. Whenever you encounter white water that you are not sure about shooting safely, portage. If there is any doubt — even the very slightest doubt — portage. Sure, portages take time and are often hard work, but they are

If your canoe doesn't have a carrying yoke, then lash the paddles so that they ride on your shoulders. This makes the canoe easier to carry over portages of some length.

90

always safer. And if the rapids are rock-studded, portaging is also easier on the canoe. This does not mean that you have to portage around every rapid. If it can be tracked or paddled, by all means do so.

On long canoe trips, portages are frequently a welcome respite from paddling, giving you a chance to work the kinks out and to stretch your legs. Along well-traveled canoe routes, portages are well marked and the trails are wide. In the wilderness, they are unmarked and often difficult to find. Always check the trail first if you have never been there before. Don't tackle the trail with a canoe on your shoulders, and then discover to your horror that it's the wrong trail. Refer to your map and compass before exploring any portage trail.

Here is the routine to follow: On landing, unload the canoe and bring it up onto shore. (We always pile the gear together.) Next, check out the portage — at least the first hundred yards or so — to make sure it's the right one. Then, tackle the portaging.

Canoes up to 18-feet long and weighing up to about 100 pounds may be portaged by one paddler if he is in good shape. Carrying rucksacks, packsacks, tackle boxes, sleeping bags, and other gear is easy. It is the canoe that worries most paddlers. But once you have mastered the art of shouldering the craft, like most other aspects of canoeing, it, too, becomes easy.

Even today, many trappers and prospectors can portage amazing loads. For example, we know of a woman trapper who runs a trap line near the tiny Indian settlement of Winisk on the bleak coast of Hudson Bay. During her spring rounds, this woman does not hesitate to tackle ¼-mile portages with a 15-foot canoe and a packsack, traps, and furs, all in one load. And when we saw her do it she was 90 years old!

If your canoe is equipped with a built-in portaging or carrying yoke, then all you have to do is shoulder it and take off. If not, for long portages, lash the paddles to the mid thwart and bow seat as shown in our photograph. On short portages of less than half a mile, many canoeists do not bother lashing paddles on. We let the mid thwart act as a yoke, while the arms are extended along the gunwales to provide balance. A cushion or wool shirt on the shoulder eases the cutting effect of the thwart.

Getting a heavy canoe up onto the shoulders can be tricky, especially if you are alone. Here is how to do it: Bring the canoe onto level ground, if possible. Point the bow in the direction you wish to go. Have the canoe resting on its keel. Stand beside it amidship, and tip it onto its side with the keel resting against your legs. Now, bend down slightly, reach across with one hand about two thirds across the centre thwart, and get a firm grip. At the same time, ease the knee well under the keel and lift up on the thwart. This movement will get the canoe off the ground and up onto your knee (actually the gunwale should be resting about four inches above the knee). Next, reach over with the other hand and grasp the thwart near the opposite gunwale. At the same time, slide the hand that originally lifted the canoe down the thwart until it is next to the gunwale resting on your knee. At this point you will be facing halfway toward the stern. Now, heave the canoe up onto your shoulders. At the same time roll your shoulders towards the bow as you lift. Your knees should straighten up only after the canoe has been shouldered. As with paddling, all movements should be deliberate but rhythmical. The act of lifting the canoe may seem a bit awkward at first, but it is not as difficult as it seems. However, it does require coordination and practice.

After the canoe has been shouldered, move the hands forward along the gunwales and shift it either backwards or forwards until you feel it is balanced. Let go with both hands (slowly) to see if it stays reasonably level. Readjust, if necessary.

Canoes are usually carried with both arms extended forward slightly and the hands grasping the opposite gunwales or the forward thwart or both sides of the bow seat. A canoe, perfectly balanced for portaging, should ride on your shoulders so that the bow is about a foot higher than the stern. This angle makes it much easier to see where you are going.

Canoes may also be shouldered by turning them over, and manhandling the bow up onto a limb or leaning it against a tree trunk. The method, in this case, is to get under the canoe, come up under the yoke, and lift the canoe. If you try this, be sure to lift with the knees, not with the back. This method is fairly easy

Canoes are carried with both arms extended slightly forward and hands holding the gunwales.

when there are two paddlers. One can hold the bow aloft, while the other gets a grip underneath. As soon as the carrier gets a grip, the other lifts the stern and helps to adjust the balance.

To lower the canoe, simply reverse the procedure for shouldering a canoe. You will find, after some practice, that you can actually rest the canoe on one knee before laying it down. Be careful not to let the canoe slip and fall. Also, avoid putting it down on rocks or stumps.

If the portage is a long one, rest once in a while. Some well-traveled portages even have rest stops with poles between trees for propping the canoe. Do not over exert yourself. It is better to stop for a rest than to try to make long portages in one lift. Tired packers are more prone to accidents than rested ones. Also, if the trail is rough, rocky, and uneven, or wet from a recent shower, walk carefully. If there are two or more paddlers making the trip, it is a good idea for one to walk ahead of the person with the canoe. The leader can pick the best places to walk, warn the canoe carrier of obstructions, and be ready to help in case of emergency. Portaging, like paddling or any other aspect of canoeing, is a team effort.

93

Avoid overloads. A small packsack, providing it is not in the way, may be portaged along with the canoe. This will depend, of course, on the weight of the canoe, the weight of the packsack, and the physical shape of the carrier. Trying to carry too much, especially if you try to carry articles in your hands while carrying the canoe, often leads to problems. Always leave the hands free to handle the canoe. The canoe is your means of getting out of the bush, and you cannot afford to have anything happen to it. Make two or three trips if necessary to portage all your gear. After all, a canoe trip is not a race.

Freighter canoes that weigh in excess of 100 pounds should be portaged by two or more persons. Usually freighter canoes are carried upside down, like conventional canoes. They may be carried in line; that is, one carrier under the canoe with the front seat or forward thwart resting on his shoulders, the other similarly positioned at the stern. If there is not enough headroom, short poles may be lashed crosswise on the gunwales, both fore and aft, to provide bars for the shoulders.

Voyageur-type canoes, with the sweeping prow and stern, are normally portaged by four and sometimes even six carriers. Carriers work in pairs — two forward and two stern. On short hauls the canoe may be carried resting upside down, with the gunwales resting on the shoulders. If it is a long portage, poles that extend two feet or so on either side of the gunwales may be more comfortable.

To sum up, these are the main points to remember:

(1) make sure you have the right portage; check the map and compass
(2) survey the trail, at least 100 yards or more of it
(3) pile all the gear together; do not forget anything
(4) do not overload; leave the hands free to handle the canoe
(5) portage as a team; keep within sight of each other
(6) take frequent rest stops; do not be in a hurry
(7) respect the rights of others using portages; wait your turn
(8) do not pitch tents, build campfires, or leave litter on portages
(9) cut poles well out of sight from any portage
(10) as with other aspects of canoeing, use common sense.

94

PART III

On the Water

CHAPTER 12

Reading the Water

There is more to canoeing than being able to paddle a canoe, just as there is more to photography than knowing how to use a camera. A true canoeist is a riverman. He can look at the water and know what lies underneath. He is an outdoorsman who can glance at a sunset and tell what weather the next day will bring. But even more, a true canoeist is an adventurer, self reliant, eager to feel the paddle responding to his arms, and always wondering what the next bend around the river will bring.

Have you ever watched a stick floating down a river? There is a definite pattern in the way it reacts to the changing flow. It plunges downward in the chutes, rocks over the breakers, and swings sideways at obstructions. If the current is strong enough, it tends to duck under fallen trees. It slows down at the cross-currents, circles in the whirlpools, backs up in the eddies, and shoots straight downstream in the main channel. A free-floating canoe behaves in a similar fashion.

It makes sense to learn about flowing water. A canoeist must learn how his canoe will respond to the current. The best place to begin learning is on a river flowing at a moderate speed, perhaps five or six miles per hour, with the odd flat rapid and maybe even a few rocks or logs jutting out here and there.

When paddling downstream, to maintain control the canoe should be traveling faster than the current. Remember, it is important to keep the canoe aligned with the flow of water. By following the main channel there is a good possibility that you will be going faster than the flow near the banks. Then all you have to do is take the odd stroke and steer. Some flat rapids or channels can be run by steering alone. But, if you are like most paddlers, you will be paddling the odd stroke by reflex.

In principle, negotiating fast-flowing rivers is no different than traveling down slow ones. The major difference is time. There is less time to compensate for errors. It is essential that both paddlers be familiar with each other's paddling techniques. They must work as a team. They should agree beforehand on a set of signals for speeding up strokes, changing directions, and stopping. Also, keep the centre of gravity as low as possible. Paddling from the kneeling position is recommended.

Basically, mastering the art of paddling on rivers is a matter of experience. The more you paddle on flowing waters, the more familiar you will become with the hydraulics and behavior of water. Let us look at this hydraulic phenomenon more closely.

Channels

Water flowing downstream tends to be faster in the channel, slower at the sides (the banks). Rocks, logs, and shoots impede its speed and direction. Surface water is faster than water at the bottom. Limnologists will tell you that water is heaviest at roughly 39°F (at that temperature it will sink to the bottom, warmer water will rise to the top). When the channel of a river narrows, the water flow speeds up; as the channel widens, the flow slows down.

Most canoeists, whether from experience or instinct, try to follow the main channel when paddling downstream. This is a good habit. On a strange river with many islands it is sometimes difficult to know which is the main channel. Consult maps whenever you can. Some rivers have navigational buoys indicating which one to take. On wild rivers you may have to decide quickly which way to go. Usually, the channel that begins to drop first is the best one, because the water must level out somewhere. Alternate courses may look quieter at first, but may eventually drop off more suddenly with dangerous chutes, falls, or rapids.

A good example of this is the Bad River, a tributary of the famous French River in Ontario, Canada. Near the mouth of the Bad River a series of channels fans out around some islands and rocks. The channel in the middle starts to drop in a series of riffles; the one on the right looks smooth, and invites closer inspection, but around the bend it drops 10 feet into Georgian Bay without any warning.

We strongly advise that any river that has rapids or fast waters extending downstream as far as you can see should be inspected from a high shore before being run. You never know what will be around the next bend.

In narrow-flowing channels take a good look at the ripples or waves. If they are fairly long and even, it indicates a good depth of water, usually enough for your canoe. If the ripples are short and uneven, watch out. It often means rocks and shallow water. A large volume of water rushing through a narrow channel is normally characterized by huge breakers, caused by fast water running head on into the slower-moving water of the widening channel. Canoes without splashcovers can be swamped by these waves, unless you can slow down the canoe sufficiently to angle through them. This takes experience. If there are any doubts, portage or track. The key thing to remember is that large, even waves mean depth; short, uneven waves mean rocks and shallow water.

Bends

Meandering rivers normally have the main channel on the outside of the bend. That is where you are most apt to run into crosscurrents and eddies. As your canoe sweeps downstream in the main channel, there is a tendency for it to plunge headlong into the opposite bank at the bend. Therefore, it is wise to take the bend on the inside; providing, of course, the water is deep enough. You will still have to be on the alert for crosscurrents, and if the water is extremely fast, there may be whirlpools at the outside edge of the main flow. Good judgment is necessary to safely negotiate fast-flowing rivers with many bends.

Here is a good way to learn how to negotiate bends. Find a winding river of medium flow, perhaps five to six miles per hour. Launch your canoe, get it into the main channel, and let it go. Chances are it will head straight for the opposite bank on the first bend, and you will have to take control. On the next bend try keeping just on the inside of the main channel and parallel to the current. You can do this by slowing the canoe down, and angling the stern towards the inside of the curve. Two experienced paddlers working in unison usually have little trouble doing this, even in fast-flowing rivers. The bowman can hold the bow while the sternman rudders the canoe around the inside of the bend.

Eddies

Eddies are generally found just around bends on the opposite sides of main channels. An eddy is a stream of water flowing in the opposite direction from the main current. Eddies are also found below rocks, big bridge abutments, and other obstructions. They come in various sizes, are usually longer than wide, often with a circular motion around them. But mostly they are quiet little oases that offer a welcome respite from the rigors of paddling.

Experienced paddlers take advantage of eddies; they stop, take stock of the situation, wipe the sweat off, realign their cargo, sponge out the canoe, check the map, or just plain catch their breath. If you are in a freighter canoe with several other paddlers and the river has been particularly wild, they are ideal for looking over your gear to make sure it is all still on board. Eddies are also good spots for landing or launching a canoe.

Rocks, Boulders, and Other Hazards

Canoes should never be allowed to bang into rocks, stumps, logs, or other obstructions. But only an armchair paddler can tell you in all honesty "I've never hit anything!" It is difficult to avoid all hazards; many are hidden under the water. Others pop up when we least expect them. Yet avoiding obstructions is key. Paddling requires alertness. A knowledge of how to avoid hazards also helps.

First, one must learn to recognize the hazard. Rocks, boulders, tree stumps, log jams, bridge abutments, pilings, and other obstructions that are above the water present no problems as far as seeing them goes. Those under the surface, however, are a different kettle of fish. On well-traveled boating waters, they are marked, but on the majority of canoeing waters they are not. So what do we look for?

Flowing water that strikes an underwater object usually forms a V that is visible at the surface. There is a flow around both sides, as well as over the top of the object. The water at the surface may be formed into a wave. Remember our earlier caution: long, even waves usually mean a good depth; short, uneven ones mean shallow waters.

A single wave several feet wide, that seems to bubble up on the downstream side, indicates a log or similar object crossways of the river. Water flowing over an underwater stump is deflected both upwards and outwards and makes waves that seem to churn.

Underwater pilings are perhaps the most difficult of all obstructions to detect. If they are near the surface, a V might be noticeable. In many cases, though, they have been in the water a long time, and the ends are well rounded. So if possible, check beforehand with someone who is familiar with the river as to its hazards. Pilings are usually found on navigable waters that have been used for commerce. The large rivers such as the Ohio, Mississippi, and St. Lawrence all have underwater pilings in some stretches. Most of them, however, have been charted.

Rivers that were once used for log drives often contain boom timbers, cribbing deflectors, dam abutments, and other structures, many fallen into ruin and decay. Others still stand like the sphinx, much the same as they were when first installed. Spikes of all sizes and wire cables were also used by logging companies. Watch for them as well.

Log booms are made by chaining or wiring together long, straight softwood logs such as white pine, jack pine, or spruce. The booms are secured either to the shore or to cribbing out in the water, and are strategically located to effectively corral all logs floating downstream. The most common locations for log booms are: at the confluence of rivers; just upstream from the outlet into a lake; above chutes, falls, and dams; above known jamming areas; below dumping grounds; above jack ladders and sluiceways; at the entrance of creeks where high waters force reverse flowage; and above reaches with little or no current.

Most logging companies remove log booms when they are finished with them. Others may have been unable to retrieve them. In any event watch for them when paddling rivers that at one time served as logging highways. Look carefully to avoid hazards. There is always a chance you may be rewarded by finding logging artifacts, still attached to the boom timbers.

Cribbing deflectors may also be found on either side of the main channel within a long series of rapids. Their purpose was to deflect the water through the deepest channel, providing a natural course for logs. Logs cut 8 or 10 feet long were spiked together at the ends to form a single tier of 6 or more feet in height. The cribbing, as it is called, was anchored in place with large boulders. Most likely the timbers will have rotted away, but the boulders may still remain, piled up at the edge of the rapids. They still function in the way they were originally intended, deflecting the water into the main channel.

Floating logs, stumps, and trees also constitute a hazard for the canoeist. They usually occur in greatest numbers right after spring breakup or severe rains that cause poorly vegetated rivers to flood. Floating objects should be given a wide berth. Pass only when it is safe to do so. Similarly, floating ice should be skirted with care. Ice jams, like log jams, should be avoided. Portage around them. Floating trees, logs, stumps, and ice can stop or even crack or puncture your canoe as effectively as a boulder. Getting around them requires deliberate action and, in fast waters, perhaps even some fancy paddling.

Here is a hypothetical example. Let's say you round the bend of a medium-fast flowing river and right in the middle of the stream is a large boulder. Both paddlers should dig their paddles in hard and back-paddle until the canoe has stopped or nearly so. Next, decide which is the main channel — that is the route you want to take. Now, paddle sideways until you are clear of the boulder, and proceed downstream. At all costs, keep the canoe from swinging sideways. You will find this lateral paddling very tiring, and after you have cleared the boulder, you may want to rest a bit. This is where an eddy comes in handy.

Crosswise logs or trees should also be skirted. They do not, however, deflect the water in the same way as boulders or other solid obstructions. You must react very quickly to avoid them. Again, as with boulders, stop the canoe, paddle sideways, and proceed past them. If, by chance, you find you cannot skirt around an overhanging log or tree, do the next best thing. Hang loose, and go down backwards. You cannot go downstream sideways — the canoe will surely upset. The only alternative is to try to go down backwards. Experienced paddlers do this frequently. Practice this trick when the waters are warm — it may come in handy some day.

Shooting Rapids

The Lachine, the Chaudière, the Blue Chute — colorful names, penned by equally colorful voyageurs as they canoed westward in search of furs and riches. Each was well known to the early voyageurs. And each has claimed its share of lives. Clay pipes, ax heads, pots, and even flint-lock muskets remain where they came to rest after being spilled from a swamped canoe, in these and a thousand other cascades across this continent. Yet, we continue to challenge the same rapids. Why?

The roar of a rapids on a wild river is like a siren song. It beckons to the canoeist in the same way that the wind swirling over a mountainside lures the climber. Shooting rapids requires a great deal of skill, the ability to make split-second decisions, good equipment, and even strength. Learn the skill and get the experience on a small rapids first. Watch how the canoe behaves and how well you are able to avoid the smallest of obstructions. Learn how skilled you are at keeping the canoe aligned with the current. Plan your course first and then check how well you have followed it. Now, portage or back track the rapids and run it again. Do it several times. Soon you will become good at it. That is when you have to be on your guard. Overconfidence and cockiness are dangerous.

Rapids may vary in mood and temperament from year to year, season to season, and even from day to day. Water levels rise and fall, logs or stumps drift in, shoals shift, and channels change. A smart canoeist checks the rapids out from beginning to end each time before he shoots them. If you plan to run the

Shooting white water is a challenging sport for many canoeists who find in the roar of rapids a song they cannot resist.

same rapids in the fall that you successfully negotiated in the summer, check them out first. Do not take anything for granted.

Once you get used to shooting short, relatively flat rapids, you will want to challenge something a little more difficult. Chances are rapids will become almost a magnet for your soul. There will be no holding you back. So, welcome to the club. We recommend that no one shoot rapids without a life preserver. A splash cover and a crash helmet are also recommended.

Begin practicing on big rapids during the summer after waters have warmed up a bit. Pick out a fast-flowing river, one that is well known for its exciting rapids — the kind that are turbulent yet can be shot with reasonable skill. If possible, talk to someone who has shot them before. Next, check out the rapids first hand. Go over all the details with your partner. Agree on the best route to take. Check out your equipment: canoe, paddles, splash covers (if you need them), life preserver, ropes at bow and stern, crash helmet, and only then take a run.

If you made it, you will feel a tingling in your spine. If you did not, hang loose, don't panic, stay with the canoe if you can, and drift downstream until you can get ashore. Take stock of the situation. Find out where you went wrong and resolve to do better next time. You are neither the first nor the last canoeist to be swamped.

Shooting rapids is a personal challenge, like gliding, mountain climbing, or bullfighting. We know some canoeists who are ever searching for more difficult and more violent rapids. Others take a more casual attitude towards fast water, either shooting, tracking, or portaging, depending upon their individual skills. Still others avoid rapids like the plague, sometimes even taking the longer route home. All have one thing in common. They are all ardent canoeists and each loves the sport for a different reason. Respect individual preferences; under no circumstances should anyone be goaded into running rapids he or she is reluctant to tackle. As we have said before: if there are any doubts, portage or track. This is particularly true if you are on a canoe trip with all your gear aboard.

Rapids that have never been shot should be approached with caution and hesitation. Pre-inspection is necessary. Rapids with ledge-like ladders of giant waves, steep drops, boulders in the channel, powerful crosscurrents, boiling whirlpools, and clouds of spray should be avoided. If you find such rapids, portage. You only have one life.

Upstream Travel

Paddling upstream is quite different from going with the current. For one thing, it is much harder. It is unlikely to get a novice into as much trouble either, being much less hazardous. We know many canoeists who explore a fast-flowing river by first paddling it upstream just to check out the tricky places, and map or log the rapids that can be safely run. On many rivers in North America, canoe trips can be planned to take advantage of water direction. You can organize your trip so that you can paddle downstream on the fast rivers and upstream on the sluggish ones. A tyro may be wise to tackle these rivers vice versa.

104

It is the wise canoeist who finds out as much as he can beforehand. Weigh the alternatives; decide on how tough a trip you want; where you can start and where you want to end.

When traveling upstream on a strange river, play it by ear. Stick to the main channel whenever you can. Do not take on longer stretches of fast water than you can handle. Take care not to exhaust yourself. Take advantage of eddies, slip up on cross-currents, portage around or track through rapids.

Canoes can get upset going upstream almost as easily as going downstream. But going upstream you have the advantage, or at least you can take advantage of almost any situation. If you get part way up a particularly strong stretch of current and feel that you cannot make it all the way, let the canoe back down, and track or portage. Keep the canoe aligned with the main flow when slipping backwards. Both paddlers should be holding their paddles so as not to swing sideways.

Rivers at Night

If there is moonlight and you are familiar with the waters, go ahead and paddle to your heart's content. Paddling down a quiet river in the moonlight is still a fine way to court a girl. Paddling on a strange river at night — moonlit or not — is another matter. It should be attempted only in an emergency. Too much can go wrong. If the river has many channels you can get lost, but tipping or damaging the canoe, losing one's gear, and injury from branches, stumps, and rocks are even more likely. If you must paddle at night on strange waters, go slowly. Stop paddling every once in a while, and listen for rapids or falls ahead. As with other aspects of canoeing, use common sense.

CHAPTER 13

Waves and Winds

A properly loaded and well-handled canoe can take a surprisingly big sea. Much, of course, depends on the skill and experience of the canoeist. In the previous chapter we advised that when in doubt about safely running a rapids, portage. There is a corollary to this regarding wind and waves. If in doubt, wait the storm out. There are times, particularly in autumn, when even the large freighters that ply the Great Lakes must seek a harbor and wait out a storm. The canoeist on stormy lakes must learn to do the same.

An open-water canoeist must learn that paddling broadside to the waves, or "in the trough" as sailors say, is a risky business. It should be avoided if at all possible. A single wave could swamp you. Breaking a high headwind with big swells crashing in on the bow is also asking for trouble. It is very difficult to maintain a true course while paddling into a headwind. The secret to paddling in waves is to quarter them. But unfortunately, to quarter waves, whether paddling with the wind or against it, is easier said than done. It takes practice and good judgment.

If the waves are breaking directly on your bow, take some evasive action. The best tactic is to steer a few degrees, say 10 to 15, either to port or starboard. You will find it easier to maintain headway as you can maintain a course and at the same time quarter the waves. The same technique applies if the waves are directly astern. After a few strokes of quartering the waves you will discover that you have to control your speed or slow down a bit, to give the bow a chance to lift up before it confronts the next wave.

Paddlers caught in high waves for the first time have a tendency to paddle hard. Try to avoid this. Paddle only with sufficient force to make some headway, until you find out how the canoe handles. Then add a little more power until you are making the best use of your energy under the existing conditions.

On long swells expert canoeists paddle hard on the crest of the roll and slow down on the far side. If the going gets too tough, they head for shore and wait for better conditions. A canoe will take high waves and remain upright under extremely high winds, but if a storm overtakes you and you find that you cannot handle it, don't panic. Sit flat in the bottom of the canoe and steer towards shore. The canoe is an amazingly seaworthy craft.

Not all waves behave in the same way. In fact, they are as diverse as rapids in a river. On shallow lakes they are usually short and choppy; in deep lakes they tend to be long and rolling. Waves respond to many physical and meteorological conditions. They build up quickly on shallow lakes, but subside just as quickly when the wind goes down. It takes longer to build a sea in deep waters, but once built, it will take an equally long time before it flattens out again. Waves in channels and around islands are often broken and uneven. Waves off capes and points may be steep and irregular as the surge around bays meets onshore wind. Waves in the backwash of rocky cliffs and breakwaters are usually broken and patternless. And, finally, waves in the lee of shoals and rock outcroppings tend to be somewhat flattened out. Here is a good place to ride out a storm.

The size of the waves alone is rarely responsible for swamping a canoe. Rather it is the type of wave. For example, waves on Lake Superior up to six or seven feet high may be successfully quartered by experienced paddlers. The same size waves on Lake Erie, however, pose a serious threat. Lake Superior is big and deep. Its waves tend to be long and rolling. Lake Erie is shallow. Its waves are short, steep, and seem to churn and roll from the bottom.

Here are some useful tips for paddlers planning to tackle large, open lakes:

(1) Learn beforehand the direction of the prevailing winds.
(2) Consult topographical maps or hydrographic charts of the lake and paddle the leeward shore.
(3) Take full advantage of islands, shoals, capes, points, and other physical features.
(4) Avoid crossings of more than one hour's paddle, about five miles from either shore or island refuge, if at all possible.
(5) Plan your trip so crossings can be made in the early morning or late evening when winds are usually lighter.
(6) Never attempt a crossing when you are tired. Rest first.
(7) Bring along a small radio to catch marine weather forecasts.
(8) Play it safe. At the first sign of a storm, head for shore and wait it out.
(9) Keep on course and use your compass; check the map or chart frequently.
(10) Remember, in most regions of North America winds are usually lighter during June, a good time to plan canoe trips for big, open water.

Paddling in Harbors or Shipping Lanes

International law dictates that the ship under power must yield the right of way to one under sail or otherwise not under power. But no motorist will argue with a Mack truck, regardless of who has the right of way. The same applies to canoeing. Big boats have limited maneuverability, especially in tight places, so give them a wide berth. The same can be said for yachts, cruisers, powerboats, and even sea planes. Give them all lots of room. It also makes sense to steer clear of water skiers, trolling fishermen, dredging operations, and construction activities.

Most charts for big lakes clearly indicate the various shipping lanes for both upbound and downbound traffic. They show the position of buoys, lights, lighthouses, moorings harbors, and other navigational aids. There are rules governing the safe operations of ships in shipping lanes and elsewhere. It is recommended, therefore, that canoeists in shipping lanes or harbors obtain a copy of marine regulations designed to provide for the safe, orderly operation of boats on our waterways. Write directly to your nearest Coast Guard, Port Authority, or Harbor Commission. Once you obtain a copy of the rules, study them and familiarize yourself with the various safety requirements: what the different types and colors of buoys mean, what lights must be displayed, what to do when meeting other craft.

CHAPTER 14

Canoe Safety

Canoes, like automobiles, airplanes, or other boats and ships, are no safer than the person at the controls. Automobile drivers get into trouble when they drive too fast for road conditions; pilots get into trouble when they fly in bad weather; and boats' captains get into trouble when they disobey navigational rules. Canoeists get into trouble when they break safety rules. Break too many of the rules and sooner or later it will cost you, perhaps even your life.

Let's look at one case history. Two big freighter canoes, both equipped with outboard motors, set out one spring day a few years ago to do some brook-trout fishing on one of the creeks flowing into Hudson Bay. The distance down the coast was about 20 miles. A party of six was in one canoe, all of them local people who had lived in the area since birth. In the other canoe were two newcomers. On landing at the mouth of the creek, the local people, observing that the tide was out, pulled their canoe up onto the tundra, stuck in a sizeable pole, and secured their canoe with rope. The other two, in a hurry to begin fishing, pulled their canoe out onto the tundra, grabbed the tackle and took off. On returning several hours later, they discovered that the tide had come in and their canoe was floating about a quarter of a mile out to sea. Even worse, a strong offshore wind was pushing it rapidly towards the horizon. Despite warnings and pleadings from the other party not to, because their motor was acting up, the tyros untied the other canoe and took off after theirs. The motor ran for a bit, then quit. They began to paddle

Life jackets don't guarantee protection from drowning in the case of a canoeing accident; however, they're of no help at all if they aren't being used.

after their canoe, which by this time had been driven by gale-force winds much farther out to sea. And that was the last anyone ever saw of the two men.

Like most canoeing tragedies it could have been prevented, but too many cardinal rules were broken; four to be exact —

(1) Heed the advice of your guide. He knows the score better than anyone else

(2) Secure the canoe on shore, especially in tidal waters.

(3) Never attempt to paddle out to sea with strong offshore winds

(4) Do not risk your life for equipment, regardless of who owns it or how much it cost.

Life Preservers

Lifejackets do not guarantee survival in a canoeing accident. But they are of no help whatsoever if they are not used. Statistics show that 85 per cent of people drowned while using boats were not wearing lifejackets. So why not tie one on — just in case.

111

Prepare yourself beforehand. Attend a boat-safety course in your neighborhood. Write your local Coast Guard or Harbor Commission. Check with an expert about different types and kinds of life preservers. Find the one that suits you and will do the job. Tie it on, wade out into the water; check that it keeps you afloat with your head out of the water. Now, try swimming with it on using a side or backstroke. If you do not know how to swim, learn. Contact your local Y.M. or Y.W.C.A.

Proper care of lifejackets is essential. A worn-out lifejacket has no safety value. When the jacket is used as a seat cushion, fender, kneeling pad, or is excessively exposed to heat or sun, its fibres or foam cells break down. It loses buoyancy and becomes useless. If the jacket gets wet, hang it up to dry in the open air. Do not attempt to dry it in front of a radiator, stove, or other direct heat source. A jacket that feels wet, heavy, and fails to dry out, must be replaced.

Proper Loading Techniques

Properly loaded canoes are important for safety. Load carefully. Keep the centre of gravity low; remember six inches of freeboard amidship. Overloading is dangerous and unsafe under all conditions. If you have any doubts about the proper load for your canoe, consult the manufacturer or seek the advice of an expert.

Communication

Always talk things over with your fellow paddlers before you attempt a crossing or shoot a rapids. Agree on signals before changing sides or paddling positions. If you are in the bow, turn your head before speaking to the sternman, especially when it is windy or rough. Canoeing requires teamwork. Make sure you let each other know what you are going to do before you do it.

Rules of the Road

Learn the various rules of inland water travel. Find out what the different-colored buoys and other navigational aids look and sound like, and what they mean. For instance, when proceeding upstream, the main channel is to the right of the black buoy. Downstream it is the opposite. Bells, fog horns, and flashing lights all signify something. For information about these symbols and abbreviations on charts, write to the U.S. Army Engineer, District Lake Survey, Corps of Engineers, 630 Federal Building, Detroit, Michigan 48226. Ask for Chart #1. For Canadian hydrographic charts, write to the Canadian Hydrographic Service, 615 Booth Street, Ottawa, Ontario, Canada.

Safety Equipment

You should have on board your canoe or person at all times: waterproof matches, compass, first-aid kit, canoe-repair kit, ropes, bailing can and sponge, ax, flashlight or flares (preferably both), maps and charts, signal mirror, spare paddles, life preserver, adequate warm clothing. Include spare woolen socks, shirts, sweaters, and underwear in waterproof bags. Also, some emergency rations.

Swamped or Upset Canoes

A canoeist's definition of a swamped canoe is one that is filled with water but is still floating upright. It is sometimes possible to bail out a swamped canoe if the sea is not too rough and water is not splashing in faster than you can bail it out. The canoe, of course, has to be very buoyant, and you must have a couple of bailing cans handy and work fast. If you are close to shore, it is better to make for it, bail the canoe out a bit, haul it up, and dump it.

Upset canoes are those that have turned over. Again, if you are near shore, stick with the canoe and paddle or tow it in. But if you are way out in the open water, you have no choice but to turn the canoe right side up, bail it out, and climb back aboard. To right an upset canoe is not as difficult as it seems. However, it does require strength and you must know how to swim. Remember, all canoes float; you are safe if you hang onto them. Cold water and time are your worst enemies. If, after a few attempts, you are not able to right the canoe, give up and hang on. Do not exhaust yourself.

What to do about a swamped or upset canoe depends entirely on where the accident happens. If you are close to shore, in rivers, streams, or narrow channels off islands, canoeists can generally make shore by kicking, thus pushing the canoe forward. If you are well off shore, however, and the wind is blowing you out, you have to consider several factors. Can you right the canoe, bail it out, and paddle against the waves to the nearest shore? How cold is the water? Can you hang on this long? Are there other boats around? Is there a chance that you will be spotted? Above all, do not panic! Think things out, weigh the alternatives, and use common sense. Under most circumstances it is wise to stick with your canoe. The only exception is if the water is too cold.

What if the water *is* too cold? Canoeing accidents in the spring and fall are usually far more serious because of this. Hypothermia, the dropping of body temperature, is the enemy. It brings death by exposure to the cold. Cold water flushes body heat from the surface of the body and lowers temperature to the fatal point. When clothes get wet they lose around 90 percent of their insulating value. Cotton is the worst offender. Wool, on the other hand, loses much less than either cotton or the synthetics. Exposure in cold water is as big a danger as drowning. You must get to shore, build a fire, and dry out, the faster the better. Abandoning your canoe and swimming to shore, providing it is not too far and you are wearing a life preserver, may be justified if the water temperature is below 50°F.

Distress Signals

S.O.S. is the international distress signal. If you are shipwrecked, scratch it out in letters on a sandy beach, or print it in leafy branches or evergreen boughs, at least 10 feet high. The S.O.S. call in the wilderness is three signals of any kind: three shots evenly spaced, three bonfires evenly spaced, three whistle blasts, three flags in line, three columns of smoke, or three successive flashes with a mirror or flare. The answer to a distress

Everyone in a canoe should always wear a life preserver.

signal is two evenly spaced shots, whistle blasts, mirror flashes, or whatever signals you can use. Bonfires should be built on rock or mineral soil to prevent them from taking off and starting forest fires. Use green boughs to make lots of smoke.

Safety Tips

(1) Leave a "flight plan." Tell your family where you are going, how long you expect to be, and your approximate return date. Also, leave word with local authorities, and check with them again when you return.

(2) Portage or track around rapids or obstacles if there are any doubts about their maneuverability.

(3) Never paddle in bad weather or dangerous water conditions. Wait on shore. Better to be a day late than to take chances.

(4) Always wear an approved life preserver; test it occasionally.

(5) Wear a crash helmet when shooting rapids.

CHAPTER 15

Canoe Care, Maintenance, and Repairs

There are a number of factors that determine how much maintenance and repairs a canoe will need and how long its lifespan. The way the canoe was built, the material from which it was constructed, even the style and size are some. And, of course, lifespan is determined to a large degree by how it has been used and cared for — in and out of the water. The kind of canoeing you do and where you do it also have a bearing, as well as the repairs you may have to make. Long, arduous trips down rock-studded rivers are bound to be hard on any canoe. In contrast, paddling each summer on a quiet lake with natural beaches, coupled with proper storage, means that a canoe will last a long time.

We know trappers who have used the same canvas-covered, cedar-strip canoe for 20 years and, except for the usual scratches, the odd cracked floorboard, and weathered gunwales, it looks like it could last for another twenty. We know others who have destroyed an 18-foot aluminum canoe on its maiden voyage down a not-so-wild river.

Maintenance

A canoe, like any other boat, requires a certain amount of care and maintenance. Aluminum and fibreglass canoes, of course, do not require as much care as wood and canvas, but even they are not entirely maintenance-free. For example, all canoes should be washed inside and out after every trip. Blood, fish slime, and gas and oil soil canoes. A light waxing once or twice a year is also recommended. Some manufacturers recommend specific wax treatments in their brochures and booklets.

Canvas-covered canoes should be varnished and painted every two to four years, depending upon the amount and type of usage. Use canoe enamel and good quality spar varnish for the task. Be sure to follow the prescribed directions for removing the old varnish and for sanding, to the letter.

Storage

There is no doubt that more canoes are ruined by improper storage than by canoe trips down wild rivers. Never store a canoe, even temporarily, against the house or against a garage wall or any other place where it will be at the mercy of the weather and the kids. Inevitably it will get knocked or blown down. Likewise, do not leave it lying on the ground because people will trip over it, put things on top of it, and kids will play in it. And, of course, on the ground, wood and canvas canoes are subject to rot and mildew.

Ideally, canoes should be stored upside down in a dry place. The ceiling joists in garages and carports are excellent storage places. Any dry shed or barn is a good bet; on top of a couple of sawhorses in a basement is another. Even an apartment dweller may find room to store a canoe, securely padlocked to a chain, from the ceiling in an underground garage. Incidentally, padlocking a canoe is a good idea if you are storing it in an open carport. More than one unchained canoe has been stolen during the owner's absence.

If you have to leave or store a canoe in the bush, cut a couple of poles and sling it between two trees. Tie it down well in case of high winds. The idea is to have it off the ground, away from porcupines. No, the porcupines will not borrow it, but they sure might want to chew it where sweaty, salt-laden hands have been handling it. The same goes for paddles, even more so.

Canoes are relatively sturdy. They are certainly not as fragile as many novices think. With a bit of care, they can last a lifetime.

117

Emergency Repairs

However, regardless of how careful we are, there comes a time sooner or later when repairs have to be made. In fact, emergency repairs on trips are quite common. It is wise, therefore, to take an emergency repair kit along. Most kits come complete with directions. Every canoe-building material — aluminum, fibreglass, wood, and canvas — can be repaired one way or another.

Aluminum Canoes. Aluminum canoes appear so tough that we tend to treat them a little less carefully than we should. Dents and scratches are common. Some of the larger dents can be pounded out with a rubber hammer or cloth-enclosed wooden mallet. Tap from the inside. An ax or even a rock, suitably wrapped with cloth, can also be used.

Mending a puncture or a crack in an aluminum canoe is another matter, but sometimes it has to be done. The first step is to pound out the dent as best you can. Next, apply some epoxy around and in the break; smooth it out with a wooden chip. Now, apply an aluminum patch and cement around it with more epoxy or a similar waterproof glue. Let it harden and hope that it will last until you get to a mechanic who can rivet a permanent patch over the break.

If you have no repair kit or glue, cotton rags, stuffed into the break and sealed with spruce gum, may do the trick. If there is no spruce, use pine gum as a second choice, balsam fir as a third.

Fiberglass Canoes. Fiberglass repair kits are available at most marinas, hardware stores, and some building supply stores. If your canoe is fiberglass, carry a repair kit with you on all trips. Repairs to a fiberglass hull, particularly if it has caved in, require considerable expertise. The canoe must be completely dry before beginning. If the weather is cool, build a fire and heat the hull a bit. Fiberglass does not set well unless the temperature is around 70° F. Be sure to follow the directions on the kit carefully, and allow plenty of time for the patch to set before hitting the water.

If you have no repair kit, try spruce gum and birch bark.

There are also some good waterproof tapes on the market that might help patch things up, at least until you get out of the bush. The best we know of is Tuck Tape.

Canvas Canoes. Canvas-covered canoes are not nearly as tough and durable as aluminum or fiberglass. They also require more maintenance, but are the easiest to repair in case of emergency.

A repair kit for a canvas canoe should include a square foot of medium-weight canvas, ten feet or so of babbish (rawhide) lacing (strip leather boot laces are good), one large darning needle, a dozen 1-inch long brass screws, a dozen or so 1½-inch long brass copper-coated flat-headed nails, and one tube, 4 fluid ounces, of ambroid. Ambroid is probably the best fast-setting glue for canvas or wood available. Incidentally, it is made by the Ambroid Company Inc., Brockton, Massachusetts 02403. It can be purchased at marinas, some hardware stores, and most northern stores of the Hudson Bay Company. However, it has been our experience in recent years that clerks in modern sporting goods and hardware stores have never heard of it. Therefore, when putting a repair kit together, do it well in advance. You may find ambroid difficult to get. Also, a small roll of 2½-inch-wide waterproof tape is a useful item to include. It can be used to patch a small puncture or slit in the canvas instantly, letting you continue the trip until you have time to make more permanent repairs.

Minor repairs to the canvas may be made simply by applying a squirt or two of ambroid to the puncture. Smooth it out with a wooden chip. Allow a few minutes for the glue to set. Canvas patches can be glued in the same way. Simply cut the patch to fit all of the rip or puncture. Rough up the outside edges of where the patch is to be affixed with steel wool, jacknife, ax, or even with a sharp stone. Wipe dry and apply the ambroid. Press patch down firmly and apply more ambroid. Smooth out and let it set and dry. If you have no canvas, use a handkerchief, shirt-tail, or similar firmly woven cotton material.

Broken thwarts, seats, gunwales, and ribs may be repaired right in the bush. Make use of the materials at hand — cedar, black ash, or even poplar, if you have to. Select a small tree well

119

back from the river or portage, so it does not show, chop off the needed length, split, and whittle out the desired piece. Screw, nail, glue, or lash it in place. If you have no babbish or string for lashing, use shoelaces or spruce roots. Spruce roots, well soaked in water, make excellent lashing material. You will find them about six inches under the matted duff at the foot of spruce trees. They are easy to pull out in long pieces.

Birch bark is also an excellent repair material for a canvas-covered canoe. Large patches of birch bark may literally be sewn in place with fine spruce roots. A sharpened hardwood twig may be used to make the stitch holes. Afterwards the holes can be waterproofed with spruce gum. Apply the gum to both sides.

Birch-Bark Canoes. The day of birch-bark canoes is not completely over. There is the odd canoeist who still uses them and even makes them. Birch-bark canoes are fragile. Their owners, therefore, tend to take very good care of them.

Techniques for repairing birch-bark canoes are similar in many ways to those for canvas-covered canoes, except that no one wants to spoil the appearance of the birch-bark canoe with modern canvas, nails, and other manufactured materials. A repair kit for a birch-bark canoe should include several strips of birch bark, a few cedar slats, a couple of partially contoured ash ribs, babbish, ambroid, and perhaps some pitch tar. Purists use spruce or pine gum instead of ambroid or pitch tar.

Paddle Care

Good paddles are expensive. After a while some even acquire a sentimental value. Taking care of your paddles is just as important as looking after your canoe. There are some do's and dont's.

First of all, usage. Avoid using your paddle as a roller to slide the canoe on, or as a fish board on which to scale or fillet fish, or as a handle on which to hang the tea pail over a fire. Do not use it to pry up logs, rocks, or other obstructions.

Paddles, like canoes, are damaged more often when they are not in use. Proper storage, therefore, is important. Try to find a

120

little-used place in your garage, toolshed, attic, or closet where you can lay the paddle flat. Paddles left standing in corners, leaning against walls, or piled helter skelter among other tools and equipment are subject to warping, twisting, or even breaking. So are paddles left out in the rain, snow, or sun for any length of time.

Most aluminum paddles require little or no maintenance at all. They should, however, be stored in a safe place to avoid being bent by heavy objects dropping on them.

Paddles, like canoes, should be washed thoroughly from time to time. Wooden paddles should be inspected before the canoeing season for cracks, slivers, and frayed edges. Lengthwise cracks in the blade may be glued shut using a carpenter's furniture vise. Crosswise cracks in the shaft usually mean it is time to invest in a new paddle. Some slivers may be peeled off, rasped, and sanded down. Others may be glued back in place and sanded smooth. It depends upon the sliver — where and how large it is. If it will interfere with the position of your hands on the paddle, then you will have to do an expert job of smoothing it out after gluing.

Frayed edges around the bottom of the blade should be planed and evened out. Some canoeists go so far as to fiberglass the edges of their paddles to prevent fraying, even before they use them. This is a good idea, but take care to do a smooth job. Fiberglass kits come with complete instructions but, like everything else, you cannot beat experience. If you have never fiberglassed before, get advice from someone who has.

Holes and nicks in your paddles may be filled with plastic wood and glue, then sanded smooth. A light sanding and varnishing with a good quality spar varnish is recommended annually for most wooden paddles. Care must be taken not to varnish the knob or portion of the shaft where the hands grip the paddle. These areas must be free of either varnish or paint to prevent blisters.

Painting the blade of the paddle is a matter of personal preference. The voyageurs did it to identify the company they represented, to distinguish their particular brigade, or for personal status and recognition. Canoe clubs, paddling groups, and individual canoeists do the same thing today. There is nothing wrong with painting the blade of your paddle, but we would like to offer one note of caution: if you are buying a new paddle that has the blade already painted, check it carefully. The paint may be covering up something.

To sum up, these are the main points to remember:

(1) Do not use your paddle as anything but a paddle.
(2) Store paddles flat in a safe, dry place.
(3) Before the canoeing season check for and make repairs to cracks, slivers, and frayed ends.
(4) An annual sanding and varnishing will prolong the life of a paddle.

CHAPTER 16

Planning Makes the Difference

Planning is one of the keys to a successful trip — any trip. Just as no one would undertake an African safari or go on some other exotic trip without well-laid plans, we should not consider making a long canoe trip without a sound, detailed itinerary. Planning a canoe trip can be lots of fun. It builds up a feeling of anticipation, and often brings back memories of other trips.

Most of us, when planning a vacation abroad, do very little of the actual planning. We leave it to a travel agent. A canoe trip can be handled in the same way. There are a great many outfitters who specialize in taking people on wilderness canoe trips to northern Canada, the upper Great Lakes states, New England, and even on the rivers of the Ozark Mountains. In fact, just as a novice world traveler is wise to leave everything to a travel agent, so a novice canoe tripper should engage the services of a competent outfitter. It is a good way to learn the basics of canoe tripping. Also you do not have to invest much money into equipment in order to find out whether canoe tripping is something you really like.

After gaining a little experience, most canoe trippers prefer to plan their own trips. Somehow it just does not seem to be "your own" if someone else has done the planning for you.

The care and attention paid to details have an important bearing on the success of the trip. The length and nature of the trip determine how much planning is required and when that planning should begin.

Many wilderness canoe trippers are finding that a good way to plan a trip is to be flown in and then paddle out.

For example, a weekend canoe trip down a river that flows through an area of villages and farms can be undertaken on the spur of the moment. You may not even need a map of the river, as long as you know that it is deep enough to float your canoe. On the other hand, a three-week trip on the Albany River, all the way to its mouth on the windswept shore of Hudson Bay, requires much more planning. On such a trip you have to be self-sufficient at all times. Your equipment has to be in first-rate order. You need good maps. And you must make arrangements to get out again once you reach the wilderness post of Fort Albany.

The old cliché "it's never too early" comes close to being the truth when planning a wilderness canoe trip. For instance, many of the canoe tripping outfittters in such popular areas as the

124

beautiful Quetico wilderness area on the Minnesota-Ontario border are booked as far as a year in advance. And even if you do not intend to use an outfitter, you will find that getting maps by mail, locating someone who has made the trip before and can give you first-hand information, or perhaps even locating and hiring a guide are all time-consuming. Actually, even selecting a waterway can take time if you intend to go with a party. Conflicting opinions mean that compromises have to be reached. And the trip must be planned so that it is not beyond the capabilities of the least experienced canoeist.

Think Innovatively!

Although the canoe is a symbol of northern wilderness, there are many waterways that offer unique and interesting canoeing, but are closer to civilization. All it takes is a desire to try something new and perhaps some unorthodox thinking. Many rivers that do not flow through wilderness can be canoed. And when it comes to making camp at night, you will be amazed how easy it is to obtain permission to pitch your tent on a riverbank farm, as long as you promise not to leave any litter or trash behind. Such rivers are ideal for the tyro canoe tripper and for families with children too small for wilderness travel. They are great for toughening your muscles and for perfecting your canoeing techniques.

The same applies to some of the bigger inland lakes, including the large reservoirs of the south, the midwest, and the southwest. You can paddle along their shorelines making a circular route. Also, such lakes are ideal for sailing a canoe. Many also have campgrounds, so finding a place to camp is no problem.

On these types of trips you do not have to carry too much in the way of provisions because you can buy food more or less as you need it. And, of course, it is reassuring to know that help is not too far away if you run into trouble.

The waterways of the south have many unique and interesting canoe routes. The famed Okefenokee Swamp of Georgia is a prime example. The swamp is laced with canoe routes of from 2 to 5 days in length. In places, where no dry ground exists for pitching a tent, wooden platforms have been built. The canoe routes in the Okefenokee are well defined and marked. On the other hand, many areas of the Florida Everglades are a formidable wilderness where no one should venture without a guide. Another good canoe tripping possibility exists in the bayou country of Louisiana. The coastal marshes there have a haunting charm.

But even urban waterways offer unique possibilities. For example, the old canals, from the days of steam tugs or even earlier when barges were pulled by oxen or mules, are interesting to canoe. Frequently they are of great historic significance. More and more people are finding that these canals offer fine recreational potential. In addition, many are now publicly owned, so it is often possible to camp along their shorelines.

Some canoeists are also discovering that the waterfronts of large cities can be canoed. Such trips are, of course, different; but they prove that a canoeist can always find some water in which to paddle his canoe. We will have more to say on this in the next chapter.

How Far?

One of the most important considerations when planning a canoe trip is time and distance. Most established canoe routes for which maps and logs are available generally give some indication as to the length of the route and how long it takes to cover it. The length of time is usually given in days. This, of course, is the most useful way of measuring how long the trip will take. Distance in miles can be quite meaningless. Canoe routes of equal length in miles will not take the same length of time to paddle if one has several portages and the other has none, or, if one means paddling against the current while the other is downstream most of the way.

Experience must also be taken into consideration when deciding on a canoe trip. If you are relatively new to the sport, perhaps not yet toughened to the paddle and a little slow at pitching or breaking camp, you may find 10 miles a day to be long enough. On the other hand, experienced canoeists who do not mind being slaves to their paddles will be able to cover 30 miles of lake travel in a day.

A day's travel in most guidebooks or logs means about 8 hours of paddling at a moderate speed. If the guidebook or log states that the route will take 5 days, then you had better plan for 5 days. It is true that experienced canoeists in good physical shape may be able to cover the route in 3 or 4 days, particularly if they paddle 12 hours a day, but you have to ask yourself what the point is. We believe that there is more to canoeing than simply chalking up miles. After all, one does not go simply to paddle. One goes to see and to experience.

So plan your trip accordingly. Do not try to cut down on time, or this may induce you to take foolish chances in shooting rapids which are beyond your skill, or in crossing windy lakes instead of paddling around the shoreline. In fact, it is better to plan an extra day or two into your trip, just in case you hit bad weather and want to sit it out. This is also wise if you want to devote some time to some of your other outdoor interests such as birdwatching, rockhounding, wildlife photography, and, of course, fishing. It is also great if you just want to loaf and rest.

With extra time, you are protected if you have to make lengthy emergency repairs to your canoe or if you run into unexpectedly good fishing. Certainly on long canoe trips one should always allow extra time. There is no fixed formula for this, but we feel that a party of two or four should allow one extra day for every five on the river. A large group may want to allow two extra days in five because groups can be slow starting in the morning. Also, with large groups, there is generally a fair diversity of interests. By allowing for extra time, everyone's interests can be accommodated.

As we just stated, there is no fixed formula determining how much time should be spent on a canoe trip. There is no doubt that there are canoe trippers who enjoy chalking up miles and spending long, hard days behind the paddle. On the other hand, there are canoeists who like their days to be slow and leisurely, taking time to explore inlets and small tributaries and to make side trips. It is all up to you. There is no right or wrong way, as long as you budget your time properly.

We have been on canoe trips where 10 miles meant a hard day of bucking current and long portages, but we have also been

127

on trips where we have covered 40 miles of running a good river in an easy day. Portages take a great deal of time. In fact, most people underestimate the length of time that portages do take. Any canoe tripper who can cover a portage one-mile long in an hour, from unloading to reloading, has done about as well as can be expected.

One of the essentials when planning a canoe trip is to establish an itinerary. This is easy to do when traveling over an established route that has been fully logged. That way you can keep to a schedule. This is particularly important if you have filed a flight plan by telling your friends where you are going and how long you will be. You do not want anyone to instigate a search for you only to have the search party find you loafing up some river just because you have lost all track of time.

On a long canoe trip it is not at all difficult to lose track of days if you are relying on memory. Keeping a log book or journal helps. Everyone should keep such a record if canoeing on a seldom-traveled route or river. Even on a well-traveled canoe route, it is a good idea to keep track of days by cutting a notch in a stick or tying knots in a piece of string.

Water Conditions

Alas, there is no way that anyone can determine ahead of time what rivers will be like or how much sea there will be on lakes. Both, to a very large degree, are governed by weather. A dry summer may mean low-water levels on many rivers. And low water may mean long portages or long distances where the canoe has to be tracked because it cannot float a load plus two people. Low water may also mean slower going because extra vigilance is needed to guard against stumps, logs, and rocks.

High water may be the result of heavy rains or a late spring. Spring break-up takes longer if the spring is late or cold. High water may cause many problems, including floating debris. But even more important, a big run-off may turn a quiet, peaceful river into a raging torrent full of dangerous shoots and rapids. A high sea on lakes is caused by wind, and in some localities, winds may blow for several days, whipping lakes into dangerous waters.

Not every canoe trip needs to be an expedition into the wilderness. The waterfronts of many of this continent's cities offer unique canoeing possibilities.

About the only thing a canoe tripper can do is to go with the averages. Plan on seasonal expectancies. If the river you are planning to canoe is navigable only in the spring or fall, go then. By and large, small rivers tend to be more navigable at these times of year. This is particularly true of farmland rivers where there are no forests to hold the water from spring run-off or to release it slowly throughout the summer.

On the other hand, the big rivers of northern Canada are generally best canoed in summer, or perhaps late spring or early fall. Many do not breakup and subside until mid-May, or even later, in the very far north.

Information and Maps

One of the key points that canoe trippers frequently neglect is to research their destination. The more you find out about the area through which you will be canoeing the better you will be able to plan your trip, including what to see and do when you are not behind the paddle.

Local chambers of commerce or tourist associations in the major resort areas are an excellent source of information. They will gladly send free travel brochures on request. Some, such as in the Wisconsin and Minnesota canoe country, are even geared to requests from canoeists. If it is unfeasible to write beforehand, stop at information offices and visitors' bureaus as you drive up to where you are planning to canoe.

There is a surprising abundance of canoeing information available, free for the asking. Many of the states and Canadian provinces in traditional canoeing areas have brochures and maps of canoe routes. All states and provinces publish booklets describing their park systems. Some even have literature describing each park in detail, including canoe routes or canoeing waters.

The United States federal government also has much useful information on canoeing and camping on or near federal land. The Bureau of Reclamation operates campsites on several rivers in the western states. Information, including maps, is available free of charge from the Information Office, Bureau of Reclamation, Washington, D.C. 20240.

Regional offices of the National Parks Service, listed in Part IV of this book — The Canoe Routes — are a good source of information on canoeing in the National Parks. Maps are available showing canoe routes. Regional offices of the National Forest Service are another good source of canoeing and camping information. Regional offices of the National Wildlife Refuge system are yet another source. Wildlife refuges are always on some sort of body of water. The waters are generally too small for extended canoe trips, but they are ideal for canoeists who are also wildlife enthusiasts.

Whenever you are writing for information, be specific. Since you are interested in a canoe trip, there is no point in being sent a parcel of information on campgrounds for automobile campers. With today's printing and paper costs, literature is expensive and should not be wasted. Even the so-called free information is not really free. Someone has to pay for it — usually the taxpayer or the consumer — and that means us.

When writing, make your letters short, clear, and to the point. Clerks in most information offices are over-burdened with work. Requests for literature come in staggering numbers. So do not waste their time by making them read useless paragraphs in a long letter. Also, write early. The big deluge of mail comes just before the summer vacation season. It sometimes takes quite a while before a letter can be processed. Here is another good reason for planning early.

Writing letters for canoeing information can be shared by members of the entire family, but a large group should form a committee, whose task it is to organize letter writing and to obtain information. If you are planning a canoeing trip with your children, let them write. It is good experience for them, and makes them feel important.

Anyone contemplating a trip down a wild river, particularly one of the big rivers of northern Canada that has never been logged, should obtain and study topographical maps of the area. Topo maps are a big help in alerting the canoeist as to what lies ahead. Topographical maps for areas east of the Mississippi River are available from the Map Information Office, U.S. Geological Survey, Washington. For maps west of the Mississippi, write to the same office, but at the Federal Center, Denver, Colorado. Topographical maps of Canada may be obtained from the Map Distribution Office, Department of Mines and Technical Surveys, Ottawa, Canada.

In Part IV of this book, we have also listed other sources of maps and canoeing information. Read these over carefully. Some may prove invaluable, once you start to plan your trip.

The Nitty Gritty

There are other aspects of planning a canoe trip that should not be overlooked. For example, late spring in many areas of northern Canada means blackflies and mosquitos. If you are particularly sensitive or even allergic to biting bugs, go some other time. Late summer or early fall are good bets because bugs generally die down by that time.

If you are planning a canoe trip into the south or south-west, then mid-summer is not the best time unless you can stand plenty of heat. Paddling in strong heat can be a tortuous task.

Find out whether you need travel permits or fire permits before entering a specific area. Fire permits are usually mandatory over most of Canada if you are planning to make a campfire. The purpose of these permits is to allow forest protection authorities to keep track of fires. In this way, when a forest-fire tower reports smoke in a certain direction, the authorities have a good idea as to whether it is a campfire or perhaps a forest fire that is just starting. Building a campfire without a permit nearly always results in a stiff fine. Judges in northern Canada take forest protection seriously and come down hard on offenders.

Travel permits play a similar role, but they are also helpful in keeping track of people in case of trouble or in case someone gets lost. But their real purpose is to exercise some control over people going into wilderness areas, particularly if the forests are very dry and if the danger of forest fire is acute. In some years all travel permits are denied and forests are closed to public travel. This is done for the protection of both the public and the forests.

Both fire and travel permits can be obtained free of charge from the nearest forest ranger office. Find out well ahead of time the location of the nearest office to your jumping-off point. You will save time in this way.

If you are planning to enjoy some fishing, and that is one of the reasons why many of us go on wilderness canoe trips, then go when the fishing is good. For example, trout fishing is best on many streams in late spring or early fall, while on lakes it is better in early spring shortly after ice-out when the surface water is still cold. Once the surface water warms up, the trout go down deep. Find out when the appropriate fishing seasons start. More than one angler has planned a canoe trip for a time when fishing seasons are closed. Also, find out where you can obtain fishing licenses well ahead of time, so you don't lose time looking for it later.

132

CHAPTER 17

Group Canoe Trips

Many clubs and associations have borrowed a page from the Boy Scout manual and are organizing group canoe trips. Such trips can be lots of fun. If the group is compatible, we can think of no better way of spending a vacation than going on a group canoe trip; unless, of course, you are the kind of person who seeks solitude. Then, you must travel alone.

There is no doubt that, in many ways, any group venture requires more careful consideration of logistics and more detailed planning than a trip for a single person. The food supply alone can be tricky. Also, the more people, the higher is the chance of illness or injury, so contingency plans must be made.

The Grumman Boat Company, a leading manufacturer of aluminum canoes, offers the following advice in organizing group canoe trips.

Get Organized

Getting your heads together to plan your trip is part of the fun. The members of Mariner Troop 567 offer smart advice: "Our Troop has a motto: if we worry about things that could possibly happen *before* we go on our trip, we will have planned to handle all contingencies without worry *while* we are on our trip." It is a good rule; we recommend it.

When your group knows where it wants to go, you can select a team of leaders to direct your planning with the needs of the chosen locale in mind. This business of picking leaders may sound awfully formal, but decisions have to be made by some-body. In addition to a project director picked by popular vote, committee chairmen should be designated for such vital areas as: itinerary and navigation; training; first aid and safety; tents and equipment; packing and loading; food and cooking; and cleanup. By involving as many members as possible in different roles, everyone develops a personal stake in seeing that details are well planned and carried out.

Agree on the actual route and number of stopovers, even for lunch breaks, as well as approximate times of departure and arrival. Of course, these times and places will not be exact, but they will give your plan a foundation on which to build. After all, you cannot schedule a trip until you know who is going where, when, and for how long.

Rev Up Your Muscles!

Canoeing calls for both muscles and skills that you do not otherwise use very often. In any community, however, there are bound to be competent outdoorsmen and women who are also good canoeists. These people, often local dealers in canoes and camping equipment, are glad to share their skills and knowledge with you.

Advance training for the trip should include exercising — push-ups and sit-ups to strengthen arm, shoulder, and abdom-inal muscles — as well as practice-loading, launching, and pad-dling sessions. These will give you great confidence, as you learn the correct techniques and skills involved.

Safety and First Aid

Any activity in the woods or on the water carries with it potential danger. But safety in canoeing is largely a matter of good sense and alertness. Horseplay does not make good sense, neither does going without personal flotation devices or the appropriate first-aid supplies.

According to the Federal Safe Boating Act, there must be a personal flotation device readily accessible for each passenger in the canoe. Use the buddy system whenever you walk, hike, swim, or explore away from the group.

134

One first-aid kit for every two canoes is advisable. Each kit should include the basics, plus a bar of old-fashioned yellow laundry soap for combating poison ivy, a snake-bite kit, anti-bug lotion, and pain-relieving sprays for sunburn.

You might preface your trip by havivng a local first-aid authority speak to the group. *Basic Canoeing,* by the American Red Cross, also explains and illustrates the essentials of canoeing safety.

In Your Old Kit Bag

Any camping trip means relative self-sufficiency in the woods. You have to take along basic food, shelter, and clothing. Simplify and take as little as possible . . . both in bulk and weight.

Camping can also be a damp business and a quick rain shower or squall can keep paddlers too busy to protect bedding and clothing. Reboarding can also bring water aboard since it is essential that the canoe be afloat before boarding (which can mean wading it out a little way). It is, therefore, a must to pack everything in waterproof containers.

Clothing and Personal Items

The key is to prepare yourself, as efficiently as possible, for temperature changes and for getting wet. Here is a suggested individual clothing list for a two-night, three-day trip:

one pair of shorts	one towel
one pair of long pants	sleeping bag
one sweater or sweatshirt	ground cloth or air mattress
several cotton shirts	(if poncho not used under
several pairs of absorbent	sleeping bag)
cotton or wool athletic socks	personal toiletries
one pair of sneakers	sunhat and sunglasses
lightweight waterproof boots	suntan and mosquito lotions
poncho, raincoat, or slicker	hobby equipment
underwear	(camera, fishing rod, etc.)
one bathing suit	personal mess kit

Packing your clothes. Sunglasses, sunhat, suntan lotion, camera, and poncho should be packed in a "gaudy bag" (a brightly colored, easy-to-spot, water-resistant, zippered beach bag) and kept close at hand for use throughout the day.

Roll up all other clothing items in your sleeping bag, and then pack that in a large plastic bag. Such plastic bags can be bought for about a dime at laundromats. Large plastic garbage bags from the supermarket will also do the job. Extras should be packed for each person. A roll of plastic tape for the entire group should be provided to make a watertight seal. If your sleeping bag has its own nylon or canvas stuff bag, put it on over the plastic-wrapped sleeping bag. This protects the plastic from ripping and insures a dry sleeping bag and clothing.

If ready-made bags are not available, they can be made by the clothing and packing committee from polyethelene sheet film bought by the roll from home-repair and building-supply stores. To make seams, tape two raw edges together lengthwise several times, then tape again.

Tents and Camping Gear

Two-man tents, which can sleep three, are preferable to heavier four-man varieties. Driving tent stakes is easiest with a hand ax; a heavy rock just is not as effective. Moreover, if the weather is threatening and tents have to go up fast, it may be well to have one ax per tent rather than just one for the entire group. You are taking the ax, of course, for the obvious purpose of chopping wood; but a lightweight folding saw is often handy for cutting large branches or logs.

When cooking for a group, it is often difficult to schedule meals cooked over a wood fire, especially in misty or damp weather. Dry wood, even in a rainstorm, can, however, be taken from the woods by snagging dead branches from standing trees. Throw a weighted light line (even a shoelace) over the branch to pull it to the ground. Quick-lighting charcoal products, available at the supermarket, are one solution. But even this fairly stable fuel should be handled with care. Take along waterproof matches in a match case, both of which you can buy in a sporting goods store.

Take a cookstove when you know that woods are so dry that authorities have banned open fires. Some western camping areas forbid all open fires. A single-burner alcohol, white-gas or propane stove is good. You can actually do all the necessary cooking on it for a group of up to 25 persons.

Here is the basic gear you will need:

tents and poles
hand axes
folding shovel (trenching
  tool)
portable stove and fuel
waterproofed matches
several large aluminum pots

toilet paper and paper towels
spatulas and long-handled
  spoons
liquid detergent or soap pads
hand spotlight (one per tent)
  and extra batteries

Packing the camp gear. Be sure to keep tent poles and pegs together in sets with the tent, and lashed aboard the canoe. (If you cut poles and pegs from the woods, use dead, not living, wood.) Dirty tent pegs should not be rolled in the tent because the dirt clogs the pores of the cloth and ruins the waterproofing. Similarly, insect repellent sprays should never be used directly on tent fabric because they dissolve the waterproofing.

Stoves, axes, lanterns; all metal items which might go to the bottom of the waterway in the event of a capsize, should be lashed firmly to the canoe, or at least tethered. Stove fuel should be brought in small quantities and stored in spill-proof cans in a shady spot. Flashlight batteries can leak in hot weather and should not be packed with clothing or in sleeping rolls.

Food

Simple food, well prepared in clean pots, and plenty of it . . . these are musts for any outdoor expedition.

When you are canoeing you must also consider weight, so canned foods can be only part of your menu. As alternatives, noodles and supermarket varieties of dried foods are light to carry and provide fairly good sustenance. Milk and other dairy products should take a minor place, especially for breakfast. They can leave a fatty residue in mouth and throat, as well as make a hard-working paddler sick to the stomach. Eggs can be cooked in advance, especially for the first morning's breakfast, and eaten hardboiled. Donuts are sugary and offer quick energy, as do the

137

sugar-coated cereals. Individual cereal packs are best. Mid-morning, hard candy sour balls in fruit flavors can be allowed to dissolve slowly in your mouth. The sourer they are, the more they quench thirst.

Lunches may be prepared and packed in individual bags at breakfast-time so that each canoeist has one. Sandwiches of the peanut-butter and jelly type provide quick energy, stick to the ribs and travel best. Never use mayonnaise on sandwiches in hot weather. A plastic jug of water can be converted instantly to lemonade or fruit punch with instant powders.

Dinner should be of the one-pot variety. For example, just before stopping for the evening meal, an ample supply of ground beef can be purchased at a shore-side town. The amount should be about ⅓ to ½ pound per person, kept in the styrofoam cooler until suppertime. Or, in the cooler, bring the meat well wrapped in foil and frozen solid. It may still be frozen by suppertime.

Brown the meat in the bottom of a large pot with some diced onions. Prepare Ground Beef Stroganoff by adding one can of undiluted cream of mushroom soup per two pounds of meat; serve over crisp chow-mein noodles. Or, instead, prepare Campfire Stew by substituting undiluted vegetable soup for the cream of mushroom; serve with or without noodles.

Next night, for a change of pace, steam an ample amount of three-minute instant rice in your large pot. Then, add canned diced chicken chunks or tunafish chunks with canned peas and several cans of undiluted cream of chicken soup. Spaghetti can be made using one of the excellent dry mixes which includes pasta, sauce, and cheese in one packet. Double the amounts to feed paddle-hungry canoeists, though.

Paper plates and cups, along with plastic utensils yield the ultimate in cleanliness. Dirty eating equipment can cause upset stomachs. Pots should be scrubbed with soap pads, and/or wet sand, then rinsed and boiled to sterilize them.

Always take out what you take in. Pack up all litter in boxes and/or garbage bags and either take it home or to a designated disposal area.

Packing the Food

Non-perishables should be packed according to the day and meal in which they are to be used: "First Day's Breakfast" might be marked on the outside of the appropriate carton, for example. It is hard to find a really good substitute for small cardboard cartons for this; they can also serve as temporary garbage boxes and they can be burned easily if need be. They stack well and protect boxes of food (donuts and cookies, for example) from being crushed. However, they can get soggy, so seal them carefully in plastic. Perishables are usually bought just before the meal at which they are to be eaten and are taken to the campsite in a lightweight, inexpensive, styrofoam picnic cooler. A word of caution: styrofoam coolers are light and keep food cold, but they are extremely fragile, so do not stack other gear on top of them.

From Alberta to Wyoming, mountain lakes offer good canoeing and fishing.

CHAPTER 18

Wilderness Canoeing

A wilderness canoe trip is a unique experience. To many of us, this is what canoeing is all about, a communion between man and nature but, also, it is much more than just an exercise in aesthetics and a quest for solitude. It is a test of self-reliance and, on occasion, of self-endurance.

The success of any wilderness canoe trip is based on three requirements, or rather on the fulfilment of three requirements. The first is proper equipment. We have already discussed canoeing equipment earlier in the book, hence there is no need to do so again, but a summary might be useful.

The party must assess its needs beforehand. The first task is to select the right vehicle. For example, a light little 15-footer is not designed for the rigors of a wilderness trip. Better opt for the 17- or 18-foot fiberglass or aluminum craft built to carry 600 pounds and still allow eight inches freeboard. One spare paddle for each paddler is essential. If the journey is a long and hazardous one, a party of two canoes is a must.

Accessory gear should include the following: compasses (take a spare), life preservers, axes (take a spare), repair kit, plenty of rope, first-aid kit, insect repellant, candles or flashlight, tent, sleeping bags, cooking outfit, waterproof liners for packsacks, and, most important of all, plenty of waterproof matches or lighters with extra fluid and flints. Experienced bush travelers carry both in different places on their person, just in case.

There are a number of excellent camping books on the market today that offer much good advice on the selection of camping equipment. The backpacking boom has really helped the wilderness canoe tripper. There is now a good selection of light, compact gear, from tents to freeze-dried foods. The wise canoe tripper, particularly if he has many portages enroute, borrows a page from the backpacker and travels light.

The selection of clothing depends upon the season, geographic area, and length of the trip. Common sense would dictate that you need warmer clothes for a canoe trip in October than if you were making the same trip in late July. Likewise, clothing needs for a canoe trip on the Okefenokee Swamp of Georgia are drastically different from those needed on a trip down the Coppermine River in Canada's Northwest Territories.

For summer canoeing in the mid latitudes of this hemisphere, cotton clothing of twills, denims, and khakis is usually ample. On warm days shorts may be preferred to long trousers, if there are no insects. A hat to shade against the sun is a must. There is no shade out on the water and too much sun can be a real hazard. On the other hand, a warm sweater and a windbreaker should be on board in case of unseasonably cool days.

For fall or early spring canoeing, warmer clothing is needed. The same applies for all canoe trips into the far north. Here the accent is on wool. Woolen underwear is a must. Warm wool shirts and trousers are far superior to cotton. Down-insulated jackets are ideal because of their lightness and wind resistance. Gloves or mitts and a warm hat are also essential for canoe trips into the north country.

Type of footwear is dictated by the expected weather, rapids to be tracked, and conditions of the portages. Light canvas and rubber boating shoes are fine for summer when there are few or no portages. We think they are superior to the traditional leather moccasins. They are comfortable yet dry quickly. But for spring and fall, leather boots (especially the waterproof kind) are best. Similarly, good sturdy leather boots are needed if you have to negotiate many portages. If you expect to do much wading when tracking a canoe, then bring along a pair of canvas shoes especially for the task, even in the fall. Leather dries slowly.

Socks should match the boots and the season. Cotton, or a com-

142

bination of cotton and nylon, are fine for summer with boating shoes, but if you have much portaging to do, wool socks are best. They give more protection to the feet and absorb perspiration much better. Wool socks are also a must for spring or fall canoeing because of their warmth. For real cold-weather canoeing, double socks — inner of pure, raw silk and outer of pure wool — are unbeatable. Double socks trap a layer of air.

The best feature about wool is that it will keep you warm even when wet. That is a point that every canoeist should remember when faced with tracking his canoe in icy water. We have waded icy water in wool socks, trousers, and underwear more than once. Lastly, do not forget to bring along a good, sturdy rain suit.

Grub for a wilderness canoe trip should be well planned beforehand. With today's dehydrated and freeze-dried foods, taking enough provisions to last for four or five weeks presents no problem. The idea is to plan each meal carefully. Stick to the staples: flour, bacon, shortening, baking powder, sugar, salt, tea, and the like. Learn to bake your own bread or, better still, learn to make bannock. Avoid heavy canned goods. In many wilderness areas the menu can be supplemented by fishing. This takes time, but who is going to grudge time spent fishing.

The other two requirements are skill and stamina. No one should venture into the wilderness unless he is a fairly competent outdoorsman and canoeist. Stamina does not mean the bull strength of the wrestler. Rather, it means the ability and endurance to paddle all day, portage a canoe, track or shoot rapids, and still have plenty of energy left to make camp, cook supper, and wash dishes.

Before you take off, get into shape. Begin about six weeks in advance. Set up a program that will establish the respiro-cardio-vascular efficiency required to make your wilderness canoe trip a real pleasure. Jogging, sit ups, push ups, weightlifting, running on the spot, all will help. If the lakes and rivers in your area are frozen over, then try some exercises that simulate paddling. Visit your local Y.W. or Y.M.C.A. Swim.

Skill comes with practice and experience. We have already discussed at considerable length the basic skills of canoeing and how to attain them. We must caution, however, that you attain sufficient canoe-handling skills prior to taking off on a wilderness canoe trip. And the place to do this is on local waters.

File a Flight Plan

Just as a bush pilot files a flight plan on where he is going, how long he will be, and when he will return, so should you before venturing on any wilderness trip. The first people you should inform are relatives and friends. Tell them where you are going, how long you intend to stay, and approximately when you will be back. Write everything down, including the name of the nearest settlement, and the lakes and rivers you plan to be on. If possible, show them on the map. Give this information to at least two people.

Just before you jump off, check in with the local authorities and, if you are coming back the same way, file a flight plan with them. Park rangers, forest rangers, conservation officers, remote tourist resorts, and fishing lodges, are ideal. In northern Canada you might leave a flight plan with the manager of a remote fur trading post such as the Hudson Bay Company, or with a detachment of the famous Royal Canadian Mounted Police.

Tips for Wilderness Canoeing

(1) Get in shape well ahead of time.
(2) Find out all you can about the route. If possible, check with someone who has made the trip before.
(3) Obtain correct maps and charts for the canoe route you will be taking.
(4) Go over the plans with the rest of the crew well in advance.
(5) Make a list of equipment and check it off. Do not forget compasses, maps, charts, axes, repair kit, life preservers, and waterproof matches.
(6) File a flight plan with your family and local authorities.
(7) While enroute, work as a team.
(8) Play it safe. Portage or track if rapids look at all risky.
(9) Leave the wilderness as you find it — no litter or garbage.

(10) Keep a logbook or journal, it may be useful to others later on.

(11) Do not take firearms. Wild animals will not bother you if you do not bother them.

(12) Take your camera and lots of film.

History Made Fun

Many of the fur-trade routes of North America remain much the same as they were when first traversed by brigades of canoes under the command of Champlain, Groseillieres, La Verendrye, Thompson, McGillivray, Fraser, Mackenzie, and others. A growing number of canoeists, gratifyingly many of them young people, are digging into their history books and actually going out and retracing the paths of the original voyageurs.

What joy to take a copy of Alexander Mackenzie's journal into the field — perhaps to the Sturgeon-Weir River, called "Rivière Maligne" by the early voyageurs. The Sturgeon-weir is a tributary of the Saskatchewan, a connecting route to the Churchill River. In his journal Mackenzie called it "an almost continual rapid." Modern canoeists can experience the portages he made and named: the Pente, Bouleau, de l'Isle, d'Epinettes, Three Galets, and several others. The water currents, the vegetation, even the very pathways, have not changed much since Mackenzie first saw them and will impress even the most disinterested historian. They give depth and life to history. And to realize that so much is still unchanged, that such a legacy still exists and waits for today's canoeist, is a thrilling prospect. What a rewarding way to combine adventure, history, and physical fitness in one trip!

Want to explore one of the fur-trade routes next summer? Write directly to the Northern Stores Department, Hudson Bay Company, Winnipeg, Manitoba. This 300-year-old company has a U-Paddle Service available. It works the same way as Hertz, Avis, or Tilden — pick up a canoe at one Hudson Bay Post and leave it at another one at the end of your journey.

You do not have to retrace the entire route in one summer. Most of us only have two or three weeks of annual vacation. You can do what many canoe trippers are doing, and retrace one of the old fur-trade routes in stages of two or three hundred miles each year.

Getting the Most Out of Wilderness Canoeing

To many of us living in cities, the wilderness is much like a foreign country. And the creatures that live there have customs and habits worthy of observing, and maybe even understanding.

In much of the wilderness the best way to see what is going on is from a canoe. A canoe is a magic thing and it works its greatest magic on wildlife. Animals that would not permit a man on foot to approach within a half mile will let a man in a canoe come close enough to see the colors of their eyes. Silence and alertness are the keys to observing animals and birds in the wilderness. Practice these on your wilderness canoe trip and you cannot miss seeing wild creatures behaving naturally in their habitat.

Shorelines and streambanks are the highways for large mammals such as moose, caribou, bear, and timber wolves. Weedy bays and grassy shallows are favorite feeding areas for large herbivores such as moose and deer. Some animals — beaver, otter, mink, and muskrat are almost entirely water-oriented. Watch for them along mud banks, rocky shorelines, below rapids, and around stony islands.

Marshes house a great horde of wild creatures: geese, ducks, rails, coots, herons, sandpipers, blackbirds, and many others. Ospreys, eagles, and kingfishers are seldom far from water. Watch for them atop some solitary dead tree or high rocky ledge. Gulls and terns prefer bald or flat-topped rocky islands out in the lake to nest on. If it is the nesting season, observe them from a distance.

But seeing or hearing the different flora and fauna of the wilderness is only part of the pleasure of being in the wild. Solving little mysteries also counts — a pile of clam shells on a sand spit indicates a family of otters has lunched recently; a floating aspen or willow branch with the leaves still green and fresh usually means beavers were active the night before; floating chunks of grass roots and clippings often expose the presence of geese or ducks; overturned rocks and mangled stumps probably indicate a black bear has been through looking for termites and grubs; a barked and mutilated tag alder or balsam fir sapling

146

heralds the presence of a bull moose, and reveals that the rut is about to begin. These are but a few of the signs to look for in the wild country. We could go on and on but then there would be no mystery left. Learn to investigate signs that appear unusual. Solve a few mysteries. That is what makes wilderness canoeing so exciting.

The sounds of the wilderness are another dimension to be explored and, hopefully, understood. We know of wilderness canoeists who deliberately camp near moose-feeding shallows, and wait out the chilly twilight without a campfire just to see and hear the crash and grunt of a big bull moose coming down to feed. We know others who will wait up half a frosty September night without fire or shelter just to hear the howl of a pack of timber wolves training their pups. Whether you are under canvas or outside soaking up the last warmth of your campfire, each night offers a special kind of entertainment.

The great horned owl makes a series of hoots that sound every bit like, "Who, Who, Cooks For You." Other owls make different sounds. On many nights there are shufflings and thumps and snapping twigs that remain mysterious. Mostly, they are small creatures such as flying squirrels, bats, rabbits, and mice. But not always. Sometimes big creatures make small noises. If you have left your grub out or neglected the dishes, it could be a bear coming to steal something. Or, it could be a porcupine chewing on a sweaty-handled paddle.

On still and clear nights some creatures seem to specialize in sounds. One of these is the loon. To any wilderness traveler the sound of the loon signifies the spirit of the wilderness. It is a wild and eerie call. To us, it's the very symbol of wilderness because the loon is a wilderness bird that rarely nests on lakes clogged with motorboats. Hear a loon once and you will never forget it.

When canoeing urban waterways, even the portages offer different scenery.

148

CHAPTER 19

Canoeing Urban Waters

In Chapter 16 we mention that urban waterways offer distinctive and different possibilities for canoe trips. Let us explore this activity further. For instance, Jim and Margo Cawley's informative book *Exploring the Little Rivers of New Jersey* describes a number of that state's waterways, the Delaware, and the Raritan Canal. The Raritan is state property, and camping is permitted anywhere along the towpath. The route includes no long portages, but does have several short ones of about 150 feet around the now-inoperative locks. That makes for lots of interest and variety in levels and views of the countryside. This canoe route is only an hour from New York City, yet it retains a very real wilderness feeling, as though the surrounding area had not changed much from the days of George Washington. There are many other such canals throughout this continent that offer fine canoeing and boating opportunities for those who want to try something different.

Many of our cities were built on the sea and on lakeshores. This is not surprising. After all, the seas and rivers were the important routes of travel and transportation for centuries before the advent of railways. Many of our great cities, therefore, have big waterfronts which are fun to explore and which also offer some of the most unexploited canoe tripping on this continent.

Granted, this kind of tripping may not appeal to everyone. If you are the kind of voyageur to whom the plaintive call of a loon is the epitome of canoeing, then a canoe trip around

New York or San Francisco won't be your bag. But for some, the sound of a foghorn is an acceptable substitute. Canoe trips on city waterfronts do have their points of interest. And as this tale from the Old Town Canoe Company shows, urban waterway canoe trips are not as far removed from nature as most of us might believe.

The Old Town Canoe Company, a leading manufacturer of fiberglass canoes, has long supported new and different canoe trips. This story, "And Nature Was There" is certainly different.

And Nature Was There

Fun is not to be found . . . you bring it with you. This axiom was well illustrated recently by six adventurous men who embarked on a 120-mile, five-day canoe trip on the waters around New York City. Their reasons were: to have a good time, and to prove to themselves that nature (more or less) does exist along some of the country's busiest waterways.

After several months of chart reading and reconnoitering the shore line by auto and on foot (part of the fun), the group was ready to go.

The route meandered from its humble point of beginning under the Hutchinson River Parkway out onto Long Island Sound to Hart Island, a desolate little spot on the map where the City buries its paupers.

After a brief stop for blackberries and a confrontation with an alarmed watchman guarding we are not sure what, they continued on to Udall's Cove, forcing their reluctant canoes through a sea of mud with vigorous strokes of their paddles.

The first night was spent under the Trog's Neck Bridge in the lee of Old Fort Schuyler at the New York State Merchant Marine Academy. They awoke to a morning of hard wind and chilling rain which was the residue left by the passing of tropical storm Doria. "Three hours is plenty when you're sleeping on cobblestones" was the dry comment made by one member of the party. "I could hardly wait to get up so I could get some rest."

"We came for a good time," observed another, "and that doesn't look like fun to me," he said, pointing out across the bay where the wind was doing exciting things with the water.

150

After a hastily convened council of war, three men finally embarked for further adventures afloat while the remaining trio remained behind to move camp to a new location under one of the archways of the ninety-year-old fort. Meanwhile . . .

The drenching rain which had been coming down since daybreak soon deteriorated into a torrent. For the men afloat, the monotony of constant paddling was broken by this opportunity to demonstrate their skills with a bailing can. At one point, weather information was being broadcast. The announcer said: "This is no day to be out in any kind of a boat." This evoked the remark from one paddler, "It sounds like Ararat and Armageddon." The weather continued foul throughout the day.

As the weather cleared, the second night was also spent at Fort Schuyler, made possible by the convenience of a car-top portage.

The third day's activities began around 3 a.m. as gale force winds tore at the camp. "I felt like I was in a balloon ready to take off," remarked one of the six canoeists.

It was discovered by examining the tide tables that high water would occur at 2:48 p.m., an ideal time to attempt the negotiation of Hellgate, a treacherous stretch of water well known for its eddies and whirlpools. They passed under the Hellgate Bridge, carried along on a 5 knot current making an easy passage. Earlier they had visited the Flushing Meadows Marina at the World's Fair site. That night was shared with gnats on the deck of the old fishing schooner *Caviar* moored near the South Street Museum.

There was a pleasant paddle out along the Brooklyn shore passing under the awesome bulk of the Verrazano-Narrows Bridge which connects Brooklyn with Staten Island; then on into Gravesend Bay and continuing up the Coney Island Creek, another quagmire which defies description. Some question was raised on passing a research submarine moored in this unlikely place. No one seemed to know what it was doing up the creek.

A natural curiosity was evidenced by open faced stares from some, and blasé acceptance from others as the six voyageurs divided the 240 plus pound load into six more or less equal parts for the mile and a half portage along Atlantic Avenue before dumping the canoes inelegantly from a bridge into the waters of Sheepshead Bay.

A leisurely exploration of the marshes and coves that comprise Jamaica Bay confirmed what all had suspected from the beginning, that nature in the form of swamp grasses, a few indifferent trees, stunted from exposure to harsh winter winds, several waterfowl, and a host of enthusiastic insects still survive despite the depredations of man.

In what might be described as the reciprocal of a white water canoe race, the three canoes, one a thirty-year-old veteran and two new guide's models, all built by Old Town, carried the little band of adventurers safely through some of the most colorful waters known to exist. All this happened within the confines of New York City.

CHAPTER 20

The Nimrod's Way

From trout fishing on Maine's clear rivers to moose hunting in northern Ontario's Chee country, the canoe has served as a useful and valiant craft. It has, since its origin, always been a vessel for hunters and fishermen. Time has not affected any significant changes. The canoe is still a nimrod's craft.

Fishing from a Canoe

To a fisherman, one of the most useful attributes of the canoe lies in its unsurpassed virtues in wilderness travel. Not even a pontoon-equipped aircraft can penetrate wilderness streams and lakes as well as a canoe. An aircraft still needs a fair-sized body of water to land on, but a canoe can make its way up the tiniest of streams.

However, its versatility goes further than that. It can glide over a salmon pool far beyond where a man can wade. And with the right kind of poling or paddling, it can put an angler within casting distance of any trout or salmon lay. With a light motor mounted on a side bracket or on a square stern, the canoe can be used for trolling on ponds and streams too small for more conventional power boats. And in a swift current, it can be anchored for still fishing with a relatively light anchor.

Even if you are not a fisherman but intend to do some wilderness canoe tripping, you should learn the rudiments of angling. A few meals of fresh fish are a welcome change on any canoe trip, and they can stretch your grub supplies considerably. The

The canoe is a tremendous fishing craft. With it, an angler can reach remote streams and lakes, waters that a conventional boat could never penetrate.

154

average paddling speed of a canoe is just about the right trolling speed for a number of fish species — pike, bass, and trout, in particular. (This speed is a little too fast for walleyes, which are more apt to strike a slower-moving lure.)

Even though fresh fish can be an important supplement to your food supply, we would not recommend that anyone actually count on living off the land. Fish, and even game for that matter, always seem hard to get when you need them the most. You may be able to supplement your diet, perhaps up to 20 percent of your meals, with fish or game if in season, but do not count on more than that.

Fishing from a canoe requires teamwork. Two anglers will find it difficult to flycast from the same canoe. The backcasts are just too long, and the lines invariably tangle. Coordinating your casts so that they alternate is, of course, possible, but even that does not always work well. Sooner or later one of the anglers will stop to concentrate on what his partner is doing and a tangle will result on the backcast. Fly fishermen find it easier to take turns fishing. We have found that 30-minute stretches are fine for most of the time, except for the brief periods when the fish are really rising. Then we alternate every 15 minutes between paddling and casting.

The paddler should handle the canoe so that it turns in all directions; thus the caster can cover all fishable water without having to change position. The angler should never cast straight ahead because this will result in a backcast straight where the paddler is sitting and the paddler might be hooked.

If the canoe is long and stable, such as a 17 or 18-footer or possibly one of the extra-wide craft, such as the Sportspal, the fisherman may be able to stand up in it to cast. Casting a flyrod is a lot easier from a standing position than from a sitting one. The angler's height adds considerable distance to the cast. And on clear days in clear water, it enables the angler to see the fish far better. However, standing in a canoe should be reserved only for the more experienced canoeist-fisherman who feels very much at home in a canoe. Novice angler-canoeists should sit.

In many ways, spinning, spin-casting, or bait-casting tackle is easier to handle in a canoe than flyfishing tackle because these methods do not require the room for backcasting. Thus there is ample room for two anglers to cast simultaneously. Spinning or spin-casting tackle has other advantages. Both are easier to use than a flyrod. This is of particular benefit to canoeists who are only casual fishermen.

Like canoeing, fishing from a canoe requires coordination from its participants. When one partner hooks a fish, the other must reel in quickly so that the fish does not become tangled around his line. If the canoe is anchored, it may be necessary for him to lift the anchor rope for the same reason. He must also stand by to give his partner a hand in landing the fish. (Assistance is nearly always needed with trophy-sized fish.)

Remember to approach each pool slowly and carefully. If possible, stay in shallow water so that you do not spook fish in the pools. Watch the sun to make sure that your shadows are not cast over the pool as you approach. If the pool is shaded by trees, keep the canoe in the shadows if at all possible: it will be less visible.

Paddle or pole to each new pool as quietly as possible. Avoid hitting the gunwale with the paddle or scraping the paddle on gravel, If you are poling with a metal-tipped pole, put the pole down gently, particularly if the bottom is rocky. There is no question that fish can hear, or, perhaps more correctly, can feel the vibrations of noise. Some fish, such as brown trout or Atlantic salmon are extremely spooky. Once they have been frightened into hiding, it may take hours before they come out and are ready to take a fly.

Poling or paddling a canoe for an angler on a river requires a fair amount of skill — both canoeing skill and fishing skill. Approach all possible places that may hold fish — rocks, stumps, logs, and so on — cautiously. Keeping a canoe steady in the face of current is difficult because you must move slowly, giving your partner ample time to probe every piece of holding water with at least one cast.

If you want to stop the canoe, do not hesitate to nudge it against rocks or logs and dig in with your paddle or pole. Sometimes it is possible to grab hold of overhanging branches or half-submerged stumps or logs. On a windy lake, it is generally best to anchor the canoe and let the angler cast all around; then move a little way and re-anchor.

If you are going downstream, be careful not to stir up clouds of sediment with your pole or paddle. If possible, paddle over areas where the current sweeps the rocks clean. Rolling clouds of sediment ahead of your canoe are bound to frighten fish. For an angler, particularly a flyfisherman, the knack of poling or paddling comes only with a fair amount of experience. Some of the best practitioners are the salmon and trout-fishing guides of Maine and New Brunswick.

Treat fellow fishermen with courtesy and consideration. It does not matter whether you are wading or canoeing. It is bad manners to pole or paddle through a pool that someone may be working, without first asking his permission. Your paddling or poling, regardless of how skillfully it is done, may ruin another man's fishing.

Hunting from a Canoe

Hunters are another group of nimrods who have made extensive use of the canoe, for similar reasons. The canoe can take the hunter deep into the wilderness, into pockets of cover and forests that cannot be penetrated as easily by any other means. It enables the hunter to travel slowly and quietly, both important attributes in successful hunting. Noise frightens game, and when a hunter travels too fast he overlooks game or game signs.

The canoe is a universal craft of the Cree Indian moose guides of northern Ontario. They paddle their client-hunters slowly and quietly through marshy lakes and meadows. In many areas, moose cannot be hunted in any other way. The forest is either too thick to see them or too thick for a hunter to walk through noiselessly. Therefore, moose are hunted on water as they feed on aquatic weeds or lush forbs and shrubs along waterways.

The canoe is also an ideal craft for moose-calling during the rut. Hunters paddle silently around small bays and inlets, calling on their birch-bark horns hoping to entice a love-starved moose into the open. When a moose comes, he may slip in as quietly as a ghost or come roaring like a locomotive, crashing through the trees. There is no more exciting way to hunt them than this.

Other game species can also be hunted from a canoe. Deer come to water in the early morning and again at dusk, and the canoe allows hunters to come up silently on likely-looking bits of cover. These can then be hunted on foot.

We have hunted ducks, both over decoys on small beaver ponds and "jump shooting" on small streams, very successfully in canoes. Their big advantage here is their mobility. It is easy to pack a canoe into a distant beaver pond or marsh where other hunters seldom venture.

Indeed, we have used our canoes to get into distant grouse and woodcock covers that are generally inaccessible or too distant for hunters on foot. Many of the best woodcock covers are found along alder-covered stream banks where these long-billed game birds can probe for earthworms in the soft, moist soil. We have read articles in outdoor magazines of other hunters using their canoes for hunting everything from squirrels to woodchucks along rivers meandering through farmers' meadows.

Hunting from a canoe requires that one take extra gun-safety precautions. For example, only the man in the bow should have a loaded gun. He is the hunter, while the sternman acts as his paddler and guide. The routine regarding when to change can be worked out between them. If both partners are paddling to reach a destination, then the firearms should be unloaded and left lying flat in the bottom of the canoe. A loaded firearm in such a position would then always point at the feet of one of the two paddlers. The only time a gun should be loaded in the canoe is when it is in the bowman's hands.

Only when duck hunting over decoys should both shoot simultaneously. This is much like hunting out of any other boat. The canoe is then broadside to the raft of decoys and must, of course, be anchored both bow and stern or tied to logs, stumps, or even branches on shore. This practice not only prevents the canoe from drifting, but makes it much steadier to shoot from. It will not upset even in the face of recoil from two 12-gauge shotguns going off at the same time. While on the subject of recoil, we would like to stress that all shooting must be done from either a sitting or a kneeling position, to keep the centre of gravity low as the gun recoils.

158

A canoe that is tied or anchored is even steady enough for a retriever to work from. The dog can jump into the water without tipping the craft, particularly if the hunter-canoeist bends back a little as a counterbalance measure. Even getting the dog back into the canoe is not difficult. First, the bird is taken from the dog's mouth as he reaches the canoe. Then one man reaches over and grabs the dog, either by his leather collar or by the loose hide on the back of his neck, and pulls his front quarters over the gunwale so that the front feet hook over the side. Then the man simply puts a bit of pressure on the dog's head to give the animal counterbalance, and the dog scrambles into the canoe on his own. Meanwhile, the other partner leans the other way to counterbalance the canoe.

One word of warning. Once the dog is in the canoe, face the other way. He will immediately shake himself and splash water over everything.

When hunting with a rifle, it is important that the paddler learn to keep the canoe steady. Even a very gentle rocking motion can make aiming a rifle from a canoe very difficult. We have known hunters to miss standing moose at 40 or 50 yards. Some of them were pretty fair shots to boot, but the sternman just could not keep the craft steady.

It is, of course, imperative that both hunters learn to paddle with the hunter's stroke. (See Chapter 7.) It is also imperative to make no noise. Noise frightens game. Wood-and-canvas canoes are quieter than fiberglass or aluminum canoes, hence better for hunting.

When hunting big game, hunters must keep the wind in their favor so that the animals are not frightened by their scent. Wind direction on water is easy to watch. Just look at the waves and how the wind ripples the surface.

Color is an important consideration for a canoe used mainly for hunting. Drab colors are the best, particularly for duck hunting. Birds are not colorblind. A brightly colored canoe or one of raw aluminum is almost impossible to camouflage — about the only way to hide a colored canoe is to have a draw-cover of camouflage- or khaki-colored canvas. When you go hunting, you slip the cover over the craft.

Some canoe manufacturers recognize the importance of color. Grumman, for example, makes a canoe especially for hunters, painted with a non-glare camouflage color. For big-game hunting, color is not as important. Mammals are colorblind, and hunters may also be wearing brightly colored clothing for safety.

The canoe is also a useful craft for carrying game out of the bush. Even a moose can be quartered and paddled out with relative ease.

Up to now we have discussed only hunting with a firearm. But a canoe is equally useful for hunting with a camera. Some of the best waterfowl pictures that we have ever taken were shot from a canoe. And, because many refuges and sanctuaries ban motorized boats, it becomes an ideal craft for traveling the waterways of these places.

Canoes for wild-life photography should also be drab. In fact, the photographer-canoeist should be drably dressed or camouflaged for less visibility, particularly when photographing birds.

160

PART IV
The Canoe Routes

CHAPTER 21

Canoe Routes in the United States and Canada

Few sports have the tradition or the history of canoeing. It is this heritage that gives it its strength and richness; however, it also imparts a weakness. The early canoeists were travelers of the wilderness, and hence modern voyageurs tend to follow that tradition, frequently thinking that only wilderness waters are fit for canoeing.

Yet the landscape has changed. The times have changed. The wilderness has retreated. In fact, there are some who argue that the wilderness vanished when the first soft-drink can was tossed onto the shores of the northern rivers. We do not necessarily agree, if for no other reason than because wilderness is a relative term. Throughout this book we have tried to stress that canoeing does not require wilderness, although escaping to the wilds may well be the highlight of this outdoor sport. The art of canoeing can be practiced on any water deep enough to float a canoe.

We cannot, in one single chapter, describe the many miles of waterways that are open to the canoeist on this continent. That could not even be done in a single book. However, what we can do is give you an opinion of the canoeing possibilities, state by state, province by province, and tell you where you can get additional information.

In this chapter you will come across references to class I, II, III, IV, and V rapids. These are criteria used to classify rapids based on the intensity of their turbulence. A description of these classifications is beyond the scope of this book. For a full explanation write to the American White Water Affiliation, whose address is listed in the Appendix.

162

UNITED STATES

Alabama Alabama has a number of potential canoe waters, particularly in the northern portion of the state. Among the larger rivers, the Black Warrior and the Chattahoochee offer quiet waters, well suited for beginners. Some of the big lakes such as Bankhead, Holt, Weiss, Logan, and others created by the Alabama Power Company have potential. So do the Tennessee Valley Authority lakes such as Wheeler and Pickwick.

For more information, write to the Alabama Department of Conservation and Natural Resources, 64 North Union Street, Montgomery, Alabama 36104.

Alaska The 49th state has tremendous wilderness canoeing potential. Most of the rivers, however, are for experienced trippers only. They entail much planning and difficult conditions.

The magnificent Kenai Peninsula has an established 120-mile canoe route, called the Swan Lake Route, which goes through some exceptionally good moose country. Detailed information on this route can be obtained from the manager of the Kenai National Moose Range, Box 500, Kenai, Alaska 99611. The Bureau of Land Management (P.O. Box 2511, Juneau, Alaska 99801) has also developed a number of smaller canoe routes. For general information write to the Alaska Department of Fish and Game, Subport Building, Juneau, Alaska 99801.

Arizona Arizona will never be an outstanding canoe tripping state, but the Colorado River below Parker Dam has about 100 miles of canoeable water. Other stretches of the Colorado, including the Grand Canyon stretch, are more suited to whitewater rafting than canoeing. The Salt River to Roosevelt Lake is another bet, with some fast water in places. The Verde River offers some fine wilderness canoeing, including white water between Clarkdale and Horseshoe. The big reservoirs offer leisurely canoeing potential.

The Arizona Game and Fish Department, 222 Greenway Road, Phoenix, Arizona 85023 should be able to supply more detailed information.

Arkansas The Ozark Mountain streams of Arkansas offer some of the best canoeing on the continent. The scenic Buffalo

River is probably the best known waterway, but there are a number of other good streams. However, many of the Ozark streams have been dammed and others are threatened.

Some streams, such as the Little Missouri River, have enough white water during the spring months to be hazardous for beginners.

For general information, write to the Publicity and Parks Commission, State Capitol, Little Rock, Arkansas 72101. A good source of specific information is the Ozark Wilderness Waterways Club, P.O. Box 8165, Kansas City, Missouri. This organization also sponsors interesting canoe trips.

California California must rank as one of our top canoeing states. The water levels in its rivers vary greatly. Many are suited only to white water canoeing, not leisurely canoe tripping. Among the better known California canoe rivers are the Eel, the Navarro, the Russian, the Trinity, the American, the King's, and the Sacramento, Klamath, Scott, and Van Duzen.

California has many active canoe clubs, a number of which are affiliated with the American White Water Affiliation.

Colorado The scenic state of Colorado offers some tremendous white water canoeing, with class III and IV rapids. The Arkansas River is perhaps the best — or should we say the meanest — white water river in the state. There are a number of good waters for tyros, but none particularly well suited to a leisurely canoe trip. The Colorado White Water Association in Denver is a good source of canoeing information; while the Colorado Game, Fish and Parks Division, 6060 Broadway, Denver, Colorado 80216, should have general information for the canoeist.

Connecticut This small New England state has a number of good waters, many of them ideally suited for beginners. The Connecticut River is one; with about 70 miles of canoeable water. The Farmington River is another; with a bit of white water over its 80 miles. Other rivers are the Housatonic, the Scantic, and the Hockanum.

The Connecticut Development Commission, State Office Building, Hartford, Connecticut 06109, has canoeing information on a number of the state's rivers. The Farmington River

164

Association Inc., 24 East Main Street, Avon, Connecticut 06001, has information on the Farmington River. The best overall source, however, on Connecticut canoeing is the New England Canoeing Guide, published by the Appalachian Mountain Club, 5 Joy Street, Boston, Massachusetts 02108.

Delaware Delaware has no waters suitable for long canoe trips, but white water fans will find the Christina River a challenging stream in April. Such streams as the Murderkill, Broadkill, Indian, Appoquinimink, Little Duck, Blackbird, and a few others offer limited canoeing opportunities.

The State Development Department, Dover, Delaware 19901, publishes a map of Delaware rivers, showing access points, state parks, and highways. The Bureau of Travel Development, 45 The Green, again in Dover, publishes a canoeing pamphlet.

Florida Even knowledgeable canoe trippers rarely think of Florida as canoeing country. Yet the state has some unique waterways.

The Suwanee River, which rises in the famed Okefenokee Swamp, must rank as one of Florida's best. Other fine rivers are the St. John, the St. Lucie, the Myaka, the Apalachicola, and a number of others.

Probably the best known canoeing water in Florida is the Juniper River at Ocolo National Forest, but in reality this body of water has only limited potential. Its route is short. On the other hand, the famous Everglades, rich in wildlife, offer tremendous canoeing potential. The National Park Service maintains a number of canoe routes and artificial campsites in this marsh and swamp area for those who wish to savor a different kind of canoeing.

The Florida Game and Fish Commission, Bryant Building, Tallahassee, Florida 32304, has canoeing information on most of Florida's rivers; while the National Park Service should be contacted regarding canoeing in the Everglades National Park.

Georgia The famed Okefenokee Swamp is Georgia's best canoe water. There is a maze of canoe and boat trails through this national wildlife refuge, with artificial camping sites established for canoe trippers. The Okefenokee Swamp is a most fascinating place.

Other good canoeing waters are the Savannah River below Augusta, the Flint River, and the Altamaha in southern Georgia. Some of the large lakes such as Clark Hill, Hartwell, Lanier, and Sinclair also offer canoeing opportunities.

For general information on canoeing in Georgia, write to the Public Relations and Information Office, Georgia Department of National Resources, 270 Washington Street, Atlanta, Georgia 30334. The Coastal Plain Area Tourist Council, Box 1223, Valdosta, Georgia 31601 and the Slash Pine Area Development Council, P.O. Box 1276, Waycross, Georgia 31501 also publish canoe route booklets on their respective areas.

Hawaii We do not, unfortunately, have any information on canoeing in Hawaii. Canoeing in fresh water in this state would certainly be very limited, as Hawaii has no major rivers or lakes. But for a skilled canoeist, particularly one who likes to sail, there is plenty of salt-water potential and salt-water canoeing is certainly an old Hawaiian tradition. Native Hawaiians, like many maritime peoples, were expert sailors in their large canoes.

The only two sources of information on canoeing in Hawaii are the Hawaiian Visitors Bureau, 2270 Kalakaua Avenue, Suite 801, Honolulu, Hawaii 96815; and the Hawaii Division of Fish and Game, 530 South Hotel Street, Honolulu, Hawaii 96813.

Idaho Idaho has many wild rivers, but it is not really an ideal canoeing state. Why? Simply because many of its rivers are a bit *too* wild, with too much white water. The rubber raft is a better and safer craft here, and certainly rafting is a popular sport in Idaho.

But there is no doubt that such famous rivers as the Salmon, Snake, the Middle and North Forks of the Clearwater, the Teton, Bear, and the Kootenai all have canoeing potential in some stretches, particularly in July and August when the water level is generally lower. Those rivers stated as slow or safe for rafting might also be good bets for canoeing. The wise move here would be to scout ahead.

The Idaho Department of Commerce and Development, State House, Boise, Idaho 83707, is one source of information on water-based recreational sports in Idaho. The Forest Office, Salmon National Forest, Salmon, Idaho 83467 has a folder and map on the Salmon River.

Illinois At first glance, the Land of Lincoln may not seem like canoe country. But it has surprisingly many canoeing opportunities. The Fox River system is one top canoe spot in Illinois with close to 100 miles of navigable water. The Illinois River can be canoed for about 275 miles. Other fine rivers are the Pecatonica, the Kankakee, Iroquois, Sangamon, Spoon, Little Wabash, and Shoal Creek. The Vermillian River is probably the best wild stream in the state, with some white water.

For urban canoeing, the Illinois-Michigan Canal and Illinois-Mississippi Feeder Canal offer interesting paddling. Both are good for training tyros.

The Boating Section, Illinois Department of Conservation, 400 South Spring Street, Springfield, Illinois 62706, publishes the *Illinois Canoeing Guide* which describes all of the state's established canoe routes.

Indiana The famous Wabash River is Indiana's longest canoeing water — a trip of about 350 miles from Bluffton to the Ohio River. Both the East and West Forks of the White River also have fine canoeing potential with few portages.

There are a number of other canoe routes in Indiana, all of which run approximately 45 to 55 miles, on such rivers as the Whitewater, the Kankakee, the Mississinewa, the Pigeon, and the Eel. There are, of course, numerous shorter routes as well.

All of Indiana's canoeing streams are relatively gentle, a good bet for beginners. The Indiana Bureau of Natural Resources, Division of Water Resources, Room 699, State Office Building, Indianapolis, Indiana 46209, publishes a booklet called *Canoeing Trails in Indiana*. There is a charge of 50 cents per copy for this booklet.

Iowa Fields of tall corn seem to be a more prominent image of Iowa than canoeing waters. Yet the state has both. The Upper Iowa River is a scenic canoe stream, fed by many springs and tributaries. The Volga River is another fine canoeing water, abutted in many places by rocky cliffs.

Other canoe streams are the Shell Rock River, the Turkey River, Red Cedar, the Raccoon River, the Little Sioux, the Iowa River, and the Des Moines River. None of these has any dangerous rapids, several flow through forested country. The fastest river in Iowa, with some white water, is the Yellow River.

167

A Copy of *Iowa Canoe Trips* can be obtained from the Iowa State Conservation Commission, 300 Fourth Street, Des Moines, Iowa 50319.

Kansas The wheat fields of Kansas are interspersed with a number of fine canoeing streams. The Neosho River, south of the John Redmond Reservoir, is the longest stream. It has close to 100 miles of navigable water and a few rapids. The Verdigris River is another fine canoe stream, as is the Fall River.

Other rivers, such as the Spring, Elk, Walnut, Kaw, and Caney, offer good canoeing opportunities. So do some of the big impoundment lakes — the Milford, Wilson, and Cedar Bluff Reservoirs.

The Kansas Forestry, Fish and Game Division, Box 1028, Pratt, Kansas 67124, has information on canoeing. Another good source is the Prairie Voyageurs Canoe Club, which is associated with the American White Water Affiliation.

Kentucky The blue grass state has excellent canoeing potential. The Red River Gorge has to be one of the most scenic canal waters on this continent. The Green River is another fine stream, with white water near Liberty. The South, Middle, and North Forks of the Kentucky River are good bets. Elkhorn Creek is fine and has outstanding fishing to boot. Tygart and Kinniconick are two other canoeing waters with great potential.

The best canoe river in Kentucky may well be the Nolin, or perhaps the Salt. The latter has the rare spotted bass to tempt anglers. But the Cumberland River is Kentucky's best known canoeing water because of the annual Angel Falls Devil's Jump canoe race, held on its Big South Fork.

The Kentucky River Canoe Club, P.O. Box 986, Bowling Green, Kentucky 42101, has information on some of the state's streams. Another source of information is the Kentucky Department of Fish and Wildlife Resources, State Office Building Annex, Frankfort, Kentucky 40601.

Louisiana The coast of Louisiana is a world of unspoiled marshland. The whole southern third of the state has a great many bayous. The Atchafalaya Basin itself must rank as one of the most intriguing wetlands on this continent. In all, Louisiana has hundreds of waterways.

Yet canoeing is not well developed in the state. The potential is there but not much has been done with it. The Louisiana Wildlife and Fisheries Commission, 400 Royal Street, New Orleans, Louisiana 70130, is one source of canoeing information. The Lafayette Natural History Museum, 637 Girard Park Drive, Lafayette, Louisiana 70501, also publishes a booklet entitled *Canoeing in Louisiana,* which sells for $2.25.

Maine The pine tree state vies with Minnesota for the honor of harboring the best canoeing country on the continent. Canoe tripping is well organized, with canoe routes clearly marked, portage trails brushed out, campsites established, and a good supply of guides available for novice canoeists. It would take a book of a respectable length to fully describe Maine's many canoe routes. (The *New England Canoeing Guide* describes most of them.)

Some of the better canoe routes are the St. Croix, the Moose River, the Grand Lake—Machias River route (which has excellent trout fishing), and the Allagash Lake route. The most demanding and longest is the St. John River route, a trip of about 200 miles.

The Maine canoe routes all have wilderness character and run through deep forests. Fishing in the late spring is generally good and wildlife is abundant.

The Tourist Division of the Maine Department of Economic Development, Augusta, Maine 04330, publishes a free booklet on a number of Maine's canoe routes. It is called *Canoeing in Maine.*

Maryland Maryland has a number of rivers suitable for canoeing, but not for serious canoe tripping. The longest canoe route is the Catoctin Creek, some 45 miles in length. Other rivers for gentle canoeing are Antietam Creek and the Monocacy River, both of which are better run in the spring.

However, Maryland does have some white water. The historic Potomac River offers a run for the better-than-average canoeist between Harper's Ferry and Knoxville, and 8 miles of wild water for the experts below Brookmount Dam. This run has class V rapids.

169

The best source of information on Maryland canoeing is *Blue Ridge Voyages,* Volumes I and II, available from Blue Ridge Voyages, 1515 North Adams Street, Arlington, Virginia 22201.

Massachusetts Massachusetts has a number of canoeing rivers, some with white water up to class IV, but the potential for canoe tripping is limited. Some of the better rivers are the Housatonic, the Connecticut, the North Branch of the Westfield, the Ware River, the Quaboag, Millers, Blackstone, Taunton, and the Charles. Wildlife buffs will find the Sudbury River, with its marshes, an interesting run.

Again, the *New England Canoeing Guide* is the best source of information on canoeing in Massachusetts. The New England Electric System, 441 Stuart Street, Boston, Massachusetts 02116, has a free booklet and a map of the Connecticut River.

Michigan Michigan would certainly rank among the top ten canoeing states in the union. The Manistique River is a fine wild river of some 75 miles. It runs through some of the Upper Peninsula's top wilderness country. Another good river is the Presque Isle, which flows by the scenic Porcupine Mountains.

But Michigan can boast of many other canoe rivers, such as the Paint, Tahquamenon, Manistee, Pine, and Père Marquette. However, the most famous of Michigan canoe waters is the Au Sable River.

The Great Lakes shores also have canoeing potential, particularly the rugged coastline of Lake Superior and, of course, the very scenic Isle Royale National Park.

The best source of information on Michigan canoeing is *Michigan's Canoe Trails,* a free booklet published by the Michigan Tourist Council, Lansing, Michigan 48926.

Minnesota The gopher state harbors more than 15,000 lakes and over 13,000 miles of rivers, all of which make for outstanding canoe country. Probably the best known canoe tripping area is the Boundary Waters Canoe Area, where the Superior National Forest and Quetico Provincial Park join to form some 14,500 square miles of wilderness. The boundary waters are popular — too popular perhaps. They draw around 100,000 canoeists annually.

But Minnesota's labyrinth of lakes and rivers offers other top canoe routes as well. The Clearwater—Bearskin route, the Sawbill Loop, the Kawishiwi Loop, the Stuart and Moose Rivers route, and the St. Croix River are just a few good waters.

Canoe tripping is well organized in Minnesota. There are countless outfitters operating in the state, offering everything from simple canoe rentals to fully organized and guided trips with a professional cook in tow. The jumping-off points are Ely, Winton, and Grand Marais.

The Department of Business Development, State Capitol, St. Paul, Minnesota 55101, has information on canoe routes and outfitters. The Ely Chamber of Commerce, Community Building, Ely, Minnesota 54731 offers information on canoeing in the Quetico—Superior wilderness area.

Mississippi There seems to be no canoeing tradition in Mississippi, and hence little canoeing. But all of the state's swampy waterways offer unique canoeing possibilities. The best known canoe routes in Mississippi lie in the famed DeSoto National Forest on the Black and Beaverdam Creeks. These canoe routes are maintained by the U.S. Forest Service.

For information on the DeSoto canoe routes, write to the Supervisor, DeSoto National Forest, Jackson, Mississippi 39205. The Mississippi Game and Fish Commission, Box 451, Jackson, Mississippi 38025 might also have some general information.

Missouri Missouri has over 2000 miles of canoeable rivers. Probably the most famous of these is the Current River, some 140 miles in length. Other good rivers are the Jack's Fork, the Eleven Point, the Big Piney, the St. Francis, the Elk, the Niangua, the Huzzah, and the Gasconade.

Actually, Missouri does not have much of a canoeing tradition. The johnboat is, or was, the more common way of traveling the Ozark's rivers and several outfitters still ply this interesting trade. But canoeing has become very popular in recent years.

Marring Missouri's canoeing scene are the dammers — proposing to and actually damming up some of the finest of the Ozark streams.

Aside from the streams, some of the big reservoirs such as

Bull Shoals, Table Rock, Lake of the Ozarks, and a number of others also have paddling potential, although they are better known for their bass fishing.

The best source of information on Missouri canoeing is Oz Hawksley's *Missouri Ozark Waterways,* available for $1, postpaid, from the Division of Commerce and Industrial Development, Jefferson Building, Jefferson City, Missouri 65102. No one should plan a canoeing trip in Missouri without consulting this book.

Montana The rivers of Montana are traditionally floated with rubber rafts. There is no doubt that some of them are better suited for this sport. Kayaking, particularly as a wild water sport, is also popular in this state. But Montana has much scope for canoeing as well.

The Main Flathead River is a good bet. The Swan is another. The Marias, Dearborn, and Smith Rivers can all be canoed in places.

The Yellowstone River is canoeable, except between the Park and Emigrant, where it is too dangerous. The Big Hole River below the Divide Dam is safe for canoes, as is the Madison above Ennis. The Missouri River can also be canoed in many places. Summer, when water levels have receded, is a better time to canoe the rivers of Montana. The rapids are tamer then.

The Montana Department of Fish and Game, Helena, Montana 59601, has a free booklet entitled *Montana Boating, Floating,* while those interested in the Yellowstone should obtain a copy of *Floating, Fishing, and Historical Guide to the Yellowstone Waterways,* by Ray Burdge, 2047 Custer Avenue, Billings, Montana.

Nebraska The rolling grasslands and farm fields of Nebraska are drained by a number of rivers that offer good canoeing opportunities. The North, South, and Middle Loup Rivers can be canoed, as can the Calamus River in the Sand Hills. The Little Blue River is a good choice for tyros, along with the Elkhorn. The Republican River is good for several days of canoe tripping.

Most of Nebraska's rivers are gentle, but the Snake and the Niobrara up to Plum Creek are for experts. Some of Nebraska's large lakes such as Conestoga, Pawnee, Wagon Train, and Lewis and Clark also have canoeing potential.

The Nebraska Game and Parks Commission, State Capitol Building, Lincoln, Nebraska 68509 publishes a booklet called the *Nebraska Boating Guide* which shows some of the canoe waters.

Nevada The canoeing potential in Nevada is limited. The state does not have many canoeable streams. The Colorado River, including its big reservoirs such as Mead and Mojave, has some potential. Easy paddling can also be had in Lakes Tahoe and Pyramid, as well as a number of others. But there is little else.

The only source of canoeing information is the Nevada Department of Fish and Game, Box 10678, Reno, Nevada 89510.

New Hampshire New Hampshire canoeing waters offer the canoeist a wide range of waters, from gentle, placid flows right up to class V rapids. The Connecticut River has fine canoeing for most of its length, as does the Merrimack. There are few, if any, really dangerous rapids on either of these waterways.

On the other hand, such rivers as the Souhegan in its upper reaches, or portions of the Suncook, Contoocook, and Pemigewasset are for white water experts only. The same is true of portions of the Ashuelot. But there are a number of streams such as the Saco River, and numerous smaller ones that are a good bet for canoeists of moderate but not expert skill.

The best source of New Hampshire canoeing information is the *New England Canoeing Guide*. The Department of Resources and Economic Development, Concord, New Hampshire 03301 publishes a free booklet called *Canoeing the Connecticut River*.

New Jersey The Delaware River is New Jersey's longest canoeing water, offering some 180 miles of water. The upper portion of this historic river is particularly scenic.

Most of the other New Jersey waters are only good for a day's run, or two at the very most. Some of these rivers are the Passaic, the Hackensack, the Wanaque, the Rancocas, the Ramapo, and the Raritan, including the interesting Raritan Canal.

The Wading River offers about 25 miles of interesting canoeing through some backwoods country, while the Great Egg River has a 35-mile run.

The New Jersey Department of Conservation, State Labor Building, P.O. Box 1889, Trenton, New Jersey 08625, publishes information on a number of New Jersey canoe routes. Another good source of canoeing information is *Exploring the Little Rivers of New Jersey,* by Rutgers University Press, New Brunswick, New Jersey 08903.

New Mexico The arid state of New Mexico does not have much canoeing potential, although during the spring runoff many of the rivers offer fine wild water sport. However, all of New Mexico's major rivers — the Rio Grande, the Canadian, the Gila, and the San Juan — have some canoeable water.

The New Mexico Department of Game and Fish, State Capitol, Sante Fe, New Mexico 87401 is one possible source of canoeing information. The Albuquerque White Water Club, an associate of the American White Water Affiliation, may be a good source of canoeing information in New Mexico as well.

New York The Empire State is top canoeing country. It offers many miles of well marked, well mapped, and well conceived canoe routes. The state government actually fosters canoeing as a healthy outdoor sport.

The Adirondacks offer a number of canoe routes of up to five or six days in length. The Delaware River is good for a 70-mile run with a few class III rapids. Such streams as the Genegantslet, the Tioughnioga, the Otselic, and the Indian Rivers offer fine novice waters of 12 to 36 miles.

Interesting and gentle canoeing can also be had in some of New York's old canals, such as the Erie Canal and the New York State Barge Canal. Even the New York City waterfront can be covered by paddlers with a yen for something different.

There is plenty of white water on a number of New York streams. The upper reaches of the Hudson River have several wild water stretches, with the wildest being near North Creek. Limestone Creek in the spring is another. Fish Creek also has wild water in places.

The New York Department of Environmental Conservation, Division of Lands and Forests, Albany, New York 122201, has free publications on many of New York State's canoe routes.

North Carolina The mountain streams of the Tarheel State offer some of the finest wild water canoeing in the south. Such rivers as the Little Tennessee, the Nantahala, and the Raven Fork have rapids up to class V, while the Green, the Pigeon, the Tuckseigee, the Toxaway, and the Ocanaluftee have rapids up to class IV.

However, there is also an abundance of gentle waters to canoe. The Catawba River chain has good potential. Much of the canoeing would be done on the lakes of this river chain. Other flat-water rivers are the Roanoke, the South, the Cape Fear, the Waccamaw, the Little Alligator, the Trent, the White Oak, the Chowan, and the Cashie.

Canoeing information on North Carolina waters is scarce. The North Carolina Wildlife Resources Commission, P.O. Box 2919, Raleigh, North Carolina 27602, is probably the only source.

North Dakota North Dakota has only a few canoeable streams. Most of the state's rivers have been dammed up, but the big reservoirs offer some paddling potential. The Red River is canoeable in many stretches, as is the Little Missouri. Early summer is the best time to try it, before the waters recede too much. The James River and the Mouse River can also be paddled, but fences across the streams can be a problem. The Turtle Mountains have a fine canoe route through a number of lakes.

The North Dakota Game and Fish Department, 2121 Lovett Avenue, Bismark, North Dakota 58501, has some canoeing information, particularly on the Turtle Mountains waterways.

Ohio The Ohio countryside is drained by a number of rivers that offer fine canoeing potential. One interesting canoe route spans 150 miles over three rivers — the Muskingum, the Walhonding, and the Mohican. The Great Miami River offers a run of about 160 miles, while the Little Miami has a run of 95 miles. The Little Miami flows through the Spring Valley Wildlife Area and the Fort Ancient State Park, giving the route additional interest.

Other good canoeing waters are the Cuyahoga, Maumee, and Sandusky Rivers. All of Ohio's canoe routes are described in *Ohio Canoe Adventures,* a free publication available from the Publication Section, Ohio Department of Natural Resources, Ohio Department Building, Columbus, Ohio 43212.

Oklahoma All of Oklahoma's major rivers have been dammed by the U.S. Corps of Army Engineers, hence the most of the state's canoeing potential is restricted to impoundments such as Lake Eufaula, Grant Lake, and Lakes Oologah, Clayton, Arbuckle, Texoma, Foss, and a number of others.

But such rivers as the Red, Washita, Canadian, and Cimarron do offer good canoeing waters, at least over parts of their courses. The best time to canoe in Oklahoma is spring and early summer, before late summer's droughts.

The best source of information on canoeing in Oklahoma is the Fish Division, Oklahoma Department of Wildlife Conservation, 1801 North Lincoln, Oklahoma City, Oklahoma 73105.

Oregon Most of Oregon's big rivers are too wild for canoeing, even by experts, but there are a few exceptions. The mighty Columbia River is one, with portaging necessary around three hydroelectric dams. The Willamette River is another. The John Day River is good in the spring and fall, but in summer it is far too low in many places.

On the other hand, such rivers as the Owyhee, the Rogue, and the Deschutes are only for the experts.

The problem with canoeing in Oregon is the lack of information on this sport. The State Tourist Department is one possible source. The Fisheries Division, Oregon State Game Commission, P.O. Box 3503, Portland, Oregon 97208 is another.

Pennsylvania Pennsylvania boasts of some superb canoeing opportunities. The streams and rivers can range from flat water flows right up to class V rapids. The Delaware River is one top canoeing water. In some stretches it offers plenty of white water, particularly in spring, but there is also enough quiet flow for beginners.

The Susquehanna River, including the West Branch, offers interesting canoeing. So do the Juniata and Lehigh Rivers. The Allegheny River is a fine river for tyros, while the Youghiogheny is an expert domain. Other Pennsylvania rivers for the expert are Black Moshannon Creek, Big Schuylkill Creek, Lolaysock Creek, and the Casselman River.

Tyros will find Kettle Creek, the Little Juniata River, Perkiome Creek, the Tioga River, and Pine Creek good bets on which to try their wings.

Unfortunately, there is little published information available.

176

The Pennsylvania Fish Commission, Box 1673, Harrisburg, Pennsylvania 17120, publishes a number of booklets on boating, fishing, and on public access points to water. A canoeist may glean something from these. A "stream map" of Pennsylvania is available for $1 from the Pennsylvania State University, College of Agriculture at University Park. A *Canoeing Guide to Western Pennsylvania* is also available from the Pittsburg Council, American Youth Hostels Inc., 6300 Fifth Avenue, Pittsburg, Pennsylvania 15232. The cost is $1.

Rhode Island The tiny state of Rhode Island does not have much canoe tripping potential, but canoeing is given a fair degree of recognition as a fine outdoor sport. The best rivers to canoe are the Pawcatuck and the Wood. The Queens River is another. The routes are well laid out, with established campsites.

Two publications of interest to canoeists are *Pawcatuck River and Wood River* and *Camping in Rhode Island* which can both be obtained free of charge from the Department of Natural Resources, Veterans Memorial Building, Providence, Rhode Island 02903.

South Carolina South Carolina offers a variety of canoeing possibilities. The Congaree River is a quiet, flat-water stream flowing through a wildlife-rich marshland. The run is about 50 miles. The Tugaloo River is another fairly gentle stream; the dams have tamed it.

The famous Chattooga River offers superb scenery and a variety of water right up to class V rapids. Such rivers as the Catawba, Wataree, and Santee also offer variety in canoeing, ranging from gentle flows to wild water.

The Broad River is a fine canoeing water. The lower portions of this river have been dammed, providing much flat water. But the upper portions have many rapids, right up to class IV.

The problem with South Carolina canoeing waters is the lack of published information. The South Carolina Wildlife Resources Department, Division of Fish, 1015 Main Street, Columbia, South Carolina 29202, is about the only possible source. For those interested in canoeing the Chattooga River, the P.T.R., Box 1358, Columbia, South Carolina 29202, has an interesting booklet.

South Dakota South Dakota has limited canoeing potential, none of which is utilized to any great extent. The best water is the Little White River which offers a run of about 110 miles. The river flows through the Rosebud Sioux Indian Reservation.

The Missouri River has been dammed and offers flat water in a number of stretches. The big impoundment lakes on the Missouri — Lewis and Clark, Francis Case, Lake Sharpe, and Lake Oahe — offer some interesting canoeing opportunities.

South Dakota also has a number of glacier lakes in the northeastern part of the state, plus other lakes in the Black Hills.

The Department of Game, Fish and Parks, State Office Building, Pierre, South Dakota 57501, is a good source of canoeing information. The Great Lakes Association, Pierre, South Dakota 57501, has information on the Missouri River impoundments.

Tennessee Tennessee, the home of country music, is also a fine canoeing state. The Buffalo River, a beautifully scenic stream, is one top canoeing water. It has a run of about 110 miles. The Harpeth River is a flat-water stream whose flow is angulated by many ox-bows. Another largely flat-water river is the Hatchie in western Tennessee.

Tennessee also has a number of white-water streams. The Obed is one with class IV rapids. The tributaries of the Cumberland — the Roaring River, Spring Creek, and Blackburn Creek — all have wild water. So do the Smokey Mountain streams such as the Hawassee, Nolichucky, and French Broad Rivers.

Tennessee also has over 20 large, man-made lakes, a number of them made by the Tennessee Valley Authority — TVA. All of them have fine canoeing potential for lake paddling and sailing.

Float maps for many of Tennessee's streams can be obtained from the Game and Fish Commission, P.O. Box 40747, Ellington Agricultural Center, Nashville, Tennessee 37203.

Texas Most of us tend to think of Texas as one huge grassland with a somewhat arid climate; hardly an image of good canoeing country. But according to Texans, the Lone Star State has everything, including canoeing waters. The Guadalupe River is one of the best in the state. The Upper Brazos is another. The Trinity River is a canoeable stream, as is the Neches.

178

The biggest river in Texas is the Rio Grande. It has much canoeing potential. The most scenic run is in Big Bend National Park, but it is for experienced canoe trippers, unless there is a guide along.

Texas also has a number of big reservoirs like Toledo Bend, Sam Rayburn, Texarkana, Buchanan, Amistad, and others.

The Texas Parks and Wildlife Commission, John H. Regan Building, Austin, Texas 78701, is one possible source of canoeing information. The American White Water Affiliation associate, the Texas Explorers Club of Temple, is even better.

Utah The Green River has become quite famous among wild-water rafters, but only a few canoeists know that it is also canoeable in many stretches. But, of course, there are impossible rapids in a number of places as well. The Colorado River is also canoeable for much of its length. The Bear River is suited to canoes in certain areas.

The easiest river to canoe in Utah is the Jordan, but even it has some white water, perhaps up to class III.

The big impoundments such as the Lake Powell on the Colorado River and the Flaming Gorge Reservoir offer interesting scenery and flat water.

The Utah Division of Fish and Game, 1596 W.N. Temple, Salt Lake City, Utah 84116, is the only source of information on canoeing in the state.

Vermont A glance at Vermont's topography or even a topographical map will tell you that Vermont must be a wild-water heaven. Vermont has a shortage of flat-water rivers. In summer, the Connecticut River tames down and becomes suitable for tyros. In spring it is mainly for experts. The Passumpsic River also offers quiet water because of dams.

Otter Creek, of the Lake Champlain watershed, is another quiet stream with a 75-mile run. The Winooski and Lamoille Rivers have mostly flat water, but both have some rapids.

The West River is Vermont's most famous wild water. The White River in the spring can offer as much challenge as any wild-water canoeist wants. The Black River also has some rapids up to classes III or IV. Other white-water streams are the Wells, Williams, Saxton's, Nulhegan, and Ottauquechee Rivers.

179

The *New England Canoeing Guide* is the best source of canoeing information on Vermont waters. But the Vermont Board of Recreation, Montpelier, Vermont 05602, publishes a free booklet, *Canoeing on the Connecticut River*. The Vermont Development Commission, Montpelier 05602, has another free booklet, *Vermont Canoeing*.

Virginia Virginia is fine canoeing country. It has rivers for canoeists of all skills and persuasions. If your bag is white water, Virginia has it. If you prefer leisurely canoe tripping, it is here too. The North and South Forks of the Shenandoah are excellent choices for canoeists of moderate skills, the South Fork being the wilder of the two. Another good river for novices is the Hazel. The Nottaway River has rapids up to class III, but generally it is easy. The Rapidan is an easy water, as is the Roanoke. The coastal streams such as the Mattaponi and the Pamunkey are all flat water. There are a number of tidal marsh streams for fishermen and wildlife buffs. Among these are the Tappahannock, Big Totuskey Creek, Gray's Creek, and Farnum Creek, to name a few.

For wild water fans the Jackson River is a good bet in the early spring, with rapids up to class V. The Hazel and Thornton Rivers have class III rapids, as does Cedar Creek. The Cheat River is class V in many places. The Cowpasture and Clinch Rivers both have many class III and IV rapids.

Canoe Trails of Eastern Virginia is a good source of information on canoeing Virginia waters. This publication is available free of charge from the Virginia Commission of Game and Inland Fisheries, P.O. Box 11104, Richmond, Virginia 23230.

Washington The rivers of Washington, like those of neighboring Oregon, are for the most part mighty torrents of water. But all of the big rivers such as the Stillaguamish, Skagit, Columbia, and Cowlitz have long stretches of quiet water.

Such smaller rivers as the Snoqualmie, Duwamish, Sammanish, Skykomish, Puyallup, Misqually, and Pilchuk all have rapids varying from class I to class IV.

The Washington Department of Fisheries, 115 General Administration Building, Olympia, Washington 98501, is one source of canoeing information. The Washington Kayak Club, associated with the American White Water Affiliation, is an even better source of information on some rivers. Signpost Publications, 16811 36th Avenue West, Lynnwood, Washington 98036, publishes a book on kayak and canoe trips in Washington. The price is $2.25, postpaid.

West Virginia West Virginia streams are mostly for white-water canoeists. The South Branch of the Potomac River is one of the best wild-water streams in the state, with a number of pitches in class IV. The smaller North Branch also has class IV water. The Great Cacapon River is a beautiful river with a number of rapids in class III. Another white-water river is the Greenbriar, with class III and IV rapids.

But there are also quiet waters in West Virginia. The Potomac is one. The North River has some rapids, but only up to Class II; thus it is a good bet for canoeists of moderate skill. A pamphlet, *Boating Facilities in West Virginia,* is a good source of information on quiet-water canoeing in the state. It is available free of charge from the Department of Natural Resources, Division of Fish and Game, 1800 Washington Street East, Charleston, West Virginia 25305.

Wisconsin Wisconsin, particularly the northern half of the state, is top canoeing country. It has a great many fine canoeing routes. The Wisconsin River Trail is a good bet for novice trippers. The Fox River is an old canoe route of the fur traders. Another fine canoe trip goes through the Waupaca chain of lakes. The Manitowish River Trail and the Turtle River are a couple more. The list could go on for several pages.

Among the waters for experts are the upper Wolf River and the Flambeau River Trail.

Canoeing is well organized in Wisconsin. The Wisconsin Department of Natural Resources, P.O. Box 450, Madison, Wisconsin 53701, publishes a booklet called *Wisconsin Canoe Trails.* It is available free on request. Indian Head Country, Inc., Route 1, Box 303, Chippawa Falls, Wisconsin 54729, publishes a number of canoeing books on Wisconsin waterways.

Wyoming Wyoming has a number of fine canoeable rivers. The Platte River is an interesting one to paddle in early summer. The Green is another good bet. The upper Greys River is suitable for paddlers with moderate skills, as is the Snake. The Lewis River in Yellowstone National Park offers fine canoeing, along with stirring scenery.

For those who want the challenge of white water, the Hoback has class III rapids. The lower Greys River has rapids in class V, and is a difficult river to run.

The Wyoming Fish and Game Commission, P.O. Box 1589, Cheyenne, Wyoming 82001, is a source of canoeing information. The Superintendent, Yellowstone National Park, Wyoming 83020, has information on canoeing in the park waters.

CANADA

Despite such large cosmopolitan cities as Montreal, Toronto, and Vancouver, Canada is still a land of seemingly endless wilderness. It also has the good fortune of having much fresh water — literally millions of lakes, streams, and rivers. Coupled with a rich canoeing tradition, Canada is truly an outstanding canoeing country.

The provincial governments are usually the best sources of canoeing information. However, the Canadian Government Office of Travel, 150 Kent Street, Ottawa, Canada K1A 0H6, also has some canoeing information, plus a useful booklet for all visitors called *So You Want to Come to Canada*.

Alberta The Athabaska River offers a 350-mile run from Jasper to Athabaska. It is not a difficult river to canoe. The Saskatchewan River can be run from Rocky Mountain House to Edmonton, about 250 miles. The Peace and the Slave Rivers offer wilderness canoeing and an opening to the Arctic watershed.

The Alberta Government Travel Bureau, 1629 Centennial Building, Edmonton, Alberta, has available a number of publications on canoeing and camping.

British Columbia Many of British Columbia's rivers are too swift and dangerous for canoeing in their entirety. But all of them — the Bella Coola, Powell, Skeena, Kispiox, Kitsumkalum, Columbia, and the mighty Fraser — offer some canoeing potential.

182

For example, the Fraser is a flat-water river for the last 110 miles before it empties into the Pacific. The North Thompson River is a fine canoeing water. The Columbia has a run of about 100 miles between Wildermere and Golden. The Peace River route, starting at Crooked River, then Pack River, and finally into the Peace, can be run right into Alberta. The Canoe River offers a pleasant 4- or 5-day trip.

The Provincial Tourist Bureau, Parliament Buildings, Victoria, British Columbia, is a good source of canoeing information.

Manitoba The big rivers of Manitoba — the Nelson and the Churchill — offer canoe trippers an excursion of a lifetime. To run one of these rivers all the way to Hudson Bay, as did fur traders of long ago, is a wilderness challenge that few of us can resist.

However, Manitoba also has easier canoe routes. The Cranberry and Wekusko Lakes route, north of The Pas, is a fine canoe trail of 120 miles. Even tyros can make it. The Whiteshell River—Winnipeg River route is another fine trip of about 100 miles through magnificent scenery. The Red River can be canoed from the U.S. border right into Winnipeg.

The Tourist Branch, 408 Norquay Building, Winnipeg, Manitoba, has free publications on all canoe routes, as well as a folder on Whiteshell Provincial Park and the Whiteshell canoe routes.

New Brunswick Canoe tripping is not a big sport in New Brunswick, yet the potential is quite good. All the major rivers — the Miramachi, the St. Croix, and St. John — offer fine canoeing. The Miramichi has a run of some 120 miles over portions of the best Atlantic salmon waters in North America.

Some of the smaller rivers such as the Restigouche and the Upsalquitch also have canoeable stretches. Although canoe tripping may not be a popular sport, the canoe is an important craft in New Brunswick. Salmon guides use it extensively for fishing.

The New Brunswick Travel Bureau, P.O. Box 1030, Fredericton, New Brunswick, has canoeing information on all the major rivers.

Newfoundland and Labrador Newfoundland has fine canoeing potential, but most of it is undeveloped. The problem is that the interior has only a few roads by which to reach the headwaters of the island's many rivers. But such rivers as the Colinet, Placentia, Trepassey, and Salmonier can all be canoed on some stretches.

The Gardner River in the north and the Highland, Fox, and New Branch Rivers in the west also offer some canoeable waters. So does the Humber River in the Northern Peninsula. All of these, incidentally, are fine salmon streams.

Labrador, a land that is mostly wilderness, has many wild rivers. The entire Churchill River watershed, the Minipi, and the Kaniapiskau have many canoeing possibilities. Labrador waters are for experienced canoe trippers only. A canoe tripper here cannot count on outside help if he gets into trouble.

The only source of canoeing information on Newfoundland and Labrador is the Newfoundland Tourist Development Office, Confederation Building, St. John's, Newfoundland.

Northwest Territories The mighty Mackenzie River is the longest run in this vast land. One can start at Fort McMurray in Alberta and canoe for some 2000 miles to the Arctic Ocean. But we recommend that anyone tackling the "Big Mac" start at Fort Smith in order to eliminate a 16-mile portage. The run from Fort Smith is about 1700 miles.

But the far north has other rivers, including the Thelon, Lockhart, Snare, Camsell, Great Bear, Laird, and Coppermine, among others. Many of these rivers cross the vast Barren Lands, home of myriads of birds, caribou, muskoxen, and the rare Barren Land grizzly.

Travel Arctic, Yellowknife, Northwest Territories, has canoeing information on all of the major rivers.

Nova Scotia Nova Scotia offers a number of interesting canoe routes suitable for novice canoe trippers. A 105-mile trip is available through the Bras d'Or chain of lakes to Lake Ainslie. There is another canoe route from Halifax to Truro through a number of lakes and canals. This run is about 75 miles.

Then there are three circular routes encompassing Alma Lake, Ponhook Lake, the Medway River, the Liverpool River, and a number of other smaller waters. Some of Nova Scotia's other rivers, such as the St. Mary's, Middle, Margaree, West, and Moser's, have stretches that can be canoed as well.

The Nova Scotia Travel Bureau, 5670 Spring Garden Road, Halifax, Nova Scotia, is the only source of canoeing information.

Ontario Ontario boasts of having more miles of developed canoe routes than all the other provinces combined. The boast may well be true. Ontario has over 250,000 lakes, plus even more rivers and streams.

Certainly the big rivers of the north — the Albany, Abitibi, and Missinaibi — offer a tremendous challenge to any canoe tripper who wants to paddle to Hudson or James Bays. Those who do not want to take on the wilderness can canoe the Trent River, the Trent Canal, Lake Simcoe, and the Severn River to Georgian Bay. That is a 175-mile run.

Algonquin Park has long been a canoe tripper's mecca, with myriads of canoe routes. But most of the 100-odd provincial parks in Ontario have some canoeing waters. Some, like Killarney Provincial Park or Superior Provincial Park, have very fine canoe trails. The Quetico Wilderness in the Boundary Waters Area is another top canoeing country. We have already mentioned it in our report on Minnesota.

Canoe tripping is well organized in Ontario. There are many outfitters who operate fully outfitted and guided trips into Algonquin Park, Quetico, and a number of other areas.

It would take a long book to describe all of Ontario's canoe routes. There are, however, a number of good sources of information. The Ontario Ministry of Natural Resources, Parks and Recreational Areas Branch, Queen's Park, Toronto, Ontario, publishes a packet of folders and maps called *Northern Ontario Canoe Routes*. They also have separate leaflets on all the provincial parks, including an extensive booklet on canoeing in Algonquin Park. The Public Relations Branch, Ministry of Industry and Tourism, 900 Bay Street, Toronto, Ontario, has a list of canoeing outfitters who provide guided trips and canoe rentals.

Prince Edward Island The tiny province of Prince Edward Island does not have much potential for canoe tripping. However, some leisurely canoeing is possible on the West, Vernon, and Morell Rivers. It is doubtful, though, that anyone would travel to Prince Edward Island to canoe. Sandy beaches, outstanding tuna fishing, and warm, hospitable people are the main attractions here. The P.E.I. Department of Environment and Tourism, P.O. Box 2000, Charlottetown, Prince Edward Island, is the best source of information on fishing and camping.

Quebec "La Belle Province" offers some enticing waters for canoe trippers. There are a number of wild rivers flowing into the Arctic watershed that challenge a canoeist. One of these is the 380-mile route from Lake Mistassini to Rupert House on James Bay via the Martin and Rupert Rivers. A number of fine wilderness canoe trails exist in the Rouyn—Noranda, Saguenay, and Temiskaming districts.

Some of the bigger Quebec Provincial Parks have well established canoe routes as well. The routes in La Verendrye Park are a good bet for tyros. Laurentide Park north of Quebec City has a number of routes as well.

A good source of information on Quebec canoe trips, particularly those in the provincial parks, is the Tourist Branch, Department of Tourism, Fish and Game, 930 St. Foy Street, Quebec City, Quebec. The Quebec Boy Scouts also have information on a number of canoe routes. Their address is Boy Scouts of Canada, 2085 Bishop Street, Montreal, Quebec.

Saskatchewan The Saskatchewan River was the early canoe route to the west, and can still be canoed by those who enjoy retracing old fur-trading routes. Prince Albert National Park has a 100-mile circular canoe route which starts and ends at Waskesiu Lake and runs through such lakes as Ajawaan, Sanctuary, Lavallee, Wabeno, Wassegam, Tibiska, Crean, and Heart.

The Churchill River offers a 240-mile run for those who want to travel through real wilderness. There is much white water on this route. Another wilderness trip takes one down the Cree River from Cree Lake to Black Lake. This, again, is a rugged trip for hardy souls.

The Extension Services Branch, Department of Tourism and Renewable Resources, Parliament Buildings, Regina, Saskatchewan has much information on canoe routes through Saskatchewan. The Superintendent, Prince Albert National Park,

Waskesiu, Saskatchewan, has information on all canoe trips in the park.

Yukon Territory   The waterways of the Yukon offer some magnificent runs through portions of the most scenic wilderness in North America. The runs are long, and generally suited only for more experienced canoe trippers.

However, the Yukon River from Whitehorse to Dawson is an easy run of smooth water. It has no portages over its 450-mile run. Anyone with only a modest amount of experience should be able to handle it, given enough time. Another fine run without portages is down the Big Salmon from Quiet Lake to the Yukon River. From there, one can paddle to Dawson City.

For those who seek a wilderness challenge, the Liard River run with a jump into the Pelly River watershed, and from there to the Yukon, should be a real trip to test strength and endurance.

The Department of Travel Information, Whitehorse, Yukon, publishes a fine booklet on the Yukon's canoe routes. A copy of *The Yukon River Log,* a reprint of old logs from the days when paddlewheelers cruised up and down the river, is well worth getting for anyone who wants to canoe down the Yukon River.

Appendix

National and Regional Information Sources

American Canoe Association, Inc.
400 Eastern Street
New Haven, Connecticut 06513

American White Water Affiliation
2019 West Addison Street
Chicago, Illinois 60618

Canadian Canoeing Association
32 Sedgewick Cres.
Islington, Ontario

United States Canoe Association
6338 Hoover Road
Indianapolis, Indiana 46260

American River Touring
  Association, Inc.
1016 Jackson Street
Oakland, California 94607

Appalachian Mountain Club
5 Joy Street
Boston, Massachusetts 02108

Minnesota-Wisconsin Boundary
  Area Commission
619 2nd Street
Hudson, Wisconsin 54016

Map Sources

U.S. Geological Survey
Washington, D.C. 20242
(for states east of the Mississippi)

U.S. Geological Survey
Federal Center
Denver, Colorado 80225
(for states west of the Mississippi)

Map Distribution Office
Department of Mines and
  Technical Surveys
Ottawa, Canada

All three of these agencies have free indexes showing the topo-graphical maps that are available for each state and province.

U.S. Army Corps of Engineers Field Offices

P.O. Box 1169
Mobile, Alabama 36601

P.O. Box 867
Little Rock, Arkansas 72203

P.O. Box 17277
Foy Station
Los Angeles, California 90017

P.O. Box 1739
Sacramento, California 95808

180 New Montgomery Street
San Francisco, California 94105

P.O. Box 4970
Jacksonville, Florida 32201

P.O. Box 889
Savannah, Georgia 31402

P.O. Box 59
Louisville, Kentucky 40201

P.O. Box 1715
Baltimore, Maryland 21203

219 Dearborn Street
Chicago, Illinois 60604

Clark Tower Building
Rock Island, Illinois 61202

P.O. Box 60267
New Orleans, Louisiana 70160

420 Trapelo Road
Waltham, Massachusetts 02154

P.O. Box 1027
Detroit, Michigan 48231

1217 U.S. P.Office & Custom House
180 E. Kellog Boulevard
St. Paul, Minnesota 55101

1800 Federal Office Building
Kansas City, Missouri 64106

906 Oliver Street
St. Louis, Missouri 63102

P.O. Box 60
Vicksburg, Mississippi 39181

6012 U.S. P.Office & Court House
Omaha, Nebraska 68101

P.O. Box 1538
Albuquerque, New Mexico 87103

Foot of Bridge Street
Buffalo, New York 14207

111 East 16th Street
New York, New York 10003

P.O. Box 1890
Wilmington, North Carolina 28402

P.O. Box 61
Tulsa, Oklahoma 74102

628 Pittock Block
Portland, Oregon 97205

Custom House
2nd & Chestnut Streets
Philadelphia, Pennsylvania 19106

564 Forbes Avenue
Manor Building
Pittsburg, Pennsylvania 15219

P.O. Box 905
Charleston, South Carolina 29402

668 Federal Office Building
Memphis, Tennessee 38103

P.O. Box 1070
Nashville, Tennessee 37202

P.O. Box 1600
Fort Worth, Texas 76101

1519 S. Alaskan Way,
South Seattle, Washington 98134

Building 602
City-County Airport
Walla Walla, Washington 99632

P.O. Box 2127
Huntington, West Virginia 25701

The following agencies have useful information on camping and canoeing on public lands under their jurisdiction:

National Offices in the United States

Office of Information
National Park Service

United States Department
  of the Interior
Washington, D.C. 20240

Information Office
United States Forest Service
United States Department
  of Agriculture
Washington, D.C. 20250

Information Office
Bureau of Reclamation
Washington, D.C. 20240

National Park Services Regional Offices

Midwest Regional Office
1709 Jackson Street
Omaha, Nebraska 68103
(402) 221-3471

Northeast Regional Office
143 S. Third Street
Philadelphia, Pennsylvania 19106
(206) 597-7018

Pacific Northwest Regional Office
523 Fourth and Pike Building
Seattle, Washington 98101
(206) 442-5201

Southwest Regional Office
Old Santa Fe Trail
P.O. Box 728
Santa Fe, New Mexico 87501
(505) 982-3375

Southeast Regional Office
3401 Whipple Avenue
Atlanta, Georgia 30344
(404) 526-7560

Western Regional Office
450 Golden Gate Avenue
Box 36036
San Francisco, California 94102
(415) 556-5186

National Capital Parks
1100 Ohio Drive, S.W.
Washington, D.C. 20242
(202) 426-6700

National Forest Regional Offices

Northern Region
Federal Building
Missoula, Montana 59801
Intermountain Region
324 - 25th Street
Ogden, Utah 84401

Southwestern Region
517 Gold Avenue, S.W.
Albuquerque, New Mexico 87101

Alaska Region
Federal Office Building
Box 1628
Juneau, Alaska 99801

Rocky Mountain Region
Building 85
Denver Federal Center
Denver, Colorado 80225

California Region
630 Sansome Street
San Francisco, California 94111

Eastern Region
633 W. Wisconsin Avenue
Milwaukee, Wisconsin 53203

Pacific Northwest Region
319 S. W. Pine Street
Box 3623
Portland, Oregon 97208

Southern Region
1720 Peachtree Road, N.W.
Atlanta, Georgia 30309

National Wildlife Refuge Regional Offices

Many National Wildlife Refuges are on water. Wildlife buffs will enjoy canoeing in the refuges.

Area Director
813 'D' Street
Anchorage, Alaska 99501
(907) 265-4868

Regional Director
Box 1306
Albuquerque, New Mexico 87103
(505) 843-2321

Regional Director
1500 Plaza Building
Box 3737
Portland, Oregon 97208
(503) 234-3361

Regional Director
Federal Building
Twin Cities, Minnesota 55111
(612) 725-3500

Regional Director
17 Executive Park Drive
   North East
Atlanta, Georgia 30329
(404) 633-9531

Regional Director
10597 West 6th Avenue
Denver, Colorado 80215
(303) 234-2209

Regional Director
John A. McCormack Courthouse
Boston, Massachusetts 02109
(617) 223-2961

PICTURE CREDITS

Thanks are due to the following organizations for the use of photographs: American Fibre-Lite Incorporated, page 111; Core Craft Incorporated, page 93; Glenbow Foundation, Alberta, page 18; Grumman Boats Incorporated, pages 42, 45, 46, 50, 76, 115; Jerome Knap, pages 56, 57, 61, 90; Notman Photographic Archives, page 13; Old Town Canoe Company, pages 2, 82, 129, 140, 148; Ontario Ministry of Industry and Tourism, pages 33, 83, 124, 154; Public Archives of Canada, pages 12, 19; Sawyer Canoe Company, pages 27, 103; Smithsonian Institute, National Anthropological Archives, page 10; Sportspal Incorporated, page 28.

Illustrations on pages 22, 23, 67, 69, 71, 73, 74, 80, and 87 by J. Hodgkinson.